A True Picture of Emigration

By
Rebecca Burlend
and
Edward Burlend

EDITED BY
MILO MILTON QUAIFE

University of Nebraska Press
Lincoln and London

First Bison Book printing: 1987
Most recent printing indicated by the first digit below:
1   2   3   4   5   6   7   8   9   10

Burlend, Rebecca.
  A true picture of emigration.

  Reprint. Originally published: New York:
Citadel Press, 1968.
  Includes index.
  1. Burlend, Rebecca. 2. Frontier and pioneer
life — Illinois. 3. Illinois — Description and
travel — To 1865. 4. Pioneers — Illinois — Biography.
5. Women pioneers — Illinois — Biography.
6. Illinois — Biography. I. Burlend, Edward, d. 1875.
II. Quaife, Milo Milton, 1880–1959. III. Title.
F545.B962 1987   977.3'4503   86-25114
ISBN 0-8032-1198-8
ISBN 0-8032-6083-0 (pbk.)

This edition reprints the Lakeside Classic published by R. R.
Donnelley & Sons Co., Chicago, in 1936.

A True Picture of
Emigration

REBECCA BURLEND

Publishers' Preface

—

THE contents of this year's volume of
The Lakeside Classics is not another
song of "arms and men." The many
preceding volumes relating hair-raising con-
flicts with the Indians and the fortitude of
the frontiersmen in the face of death from
starvation and thirst have established an
expectancy that the subject matter of the
series must have a wild west flavor. This
volume, however, moves in a more quiet
tempo. It is the story of a woman, who, with
her husband and three children, emigrated
from England in 1831 to settle in the wilds
of western Illinois. It is probably typical of
the story of hundreds of thousands of other
women who likewise followed their husbands to the new world in order that they
might improve their own condition and that
of their children; women who accepted the
privations and difficulties of the joint venture valiantly and who, when crushing disap-
pointments came, with brave hearts brought
renewed courage to their husbands to fight
through. One cannot read this simple story
without realizing that these pioneer women

did their full share in conquering the new world, nor can the thought escape one that these early farmers were of that sturdy stuff that accepted the challenge of Nature and conquered her, without the help of modern machinery, transportation, and markets, and the coddling of an indulgent government.

"A True Picture of Emigration, or Fourteen Years in the Interior of North America" was published in England in 1848. It was an insignificant pamphlet of four by seven inches, of 62 pages, printed in small type, bound in paper, and selling for 6d. It has been included for many years in the various bibliographies of early American history, but being published anonymously it was so described. The pamphlet was recommended to the publishers by Mr. Oliver R. Barrett of Kenilworth, Illinois, a life-time collector of rare books, to whom it had long been a favorite. The publishers are also indebted to Mr. Barrett for the identity of the author, the discovery of which is a pleasant story of a book collector's enthusiasm. Born in Pike County, Illinois, Mr. Barrett was familiar with the scene of this narrative and thought it possible by the study of land titles and transfers to find the name of the author. The story can best be told by the two following letters:

Publishers' Preface

March 9, 1936

Mr. Jesse M. Thompson,
Pittsfield, Illinois.

Dear Mr. Thompson:

I read your series of articles on Early Pike County with a great deal of interest. I hope they will continue for a long time to come. When your present material is exhausted, I think it would be worth while to reprint a part, at least, of the well written and interesting narrative of pioneer life in Pike County, Illinois, in 1831–1845. The title of this rare little item of Americana is:

A TRUE PICTURE

OF

EMIGRATION

OR FOURTEEN YEARS IN

THE INTERIOR OF NORTH AMERICA

BEING A FULL AND

IMPARTIAL ACCOUNT

OF THE

VARIOUS DIFFICULTIES

AND ULTIMATE

SUCCESS OF AN ENGLISH FAMILY

WHO EMIGRATED FROM

BARWICK-IN-ELMET, NEAR LEEDS,

IN THE YEAR 1831.

It was published anonymously in London about 1848, and the name of the lady author has never been discovered, although I think you will be able to identify her. She came from Yorkshire to Pike County with her husband and five children, the eldest nine years of age. (A son and daughter, both employed, were left in England.) They landed in the fall of 1831 at Philips Ferry, then a wooded shore. A little inland, they found Mr. Phillips, with whom they lived for a short period, after which they bought an 80-acre tract, which Mr. Oakes had preëmpted, and they registered this land in the Quincy Land Office.

From the book it appears that this land was a few miles from Philips Ferry and fifty miles from Quincy. Among the neighbors mentioned are Mr. Paddock, Mr. Burns, Mr. Knowles, each living about two miles from the author, and Mr. Varley, the store-keeper.

As far as I have noticed, the only settlers in that neighborhood who came from England in 1831 were James Crawford, who settled in section 19, Flint tp., and John Burlend, who came from Yorkshire (Leeds is in Yorkshire), and settled either in Flint or Detroit tp. in 1831. The facts mentioned in the book seem to indicate that the author of the book was the wife of the latter. In the book her given name is mentioned as

Publishers' Preface

"Rebecca" and that was also the name of John Burlend's wife.

From the book it appears that the author left a grown daughter in England, and that in the 40's she returned for a visit to England and when she came back from England, her daughter and her daughter's husband came with her. That daughter may have been the Mary Burlend who married Luke Yelliott, in Yorkshire, in 1840, and soon after came to Detroit tp., where her parents lived. (See History of Pike County.)

In their old age, John and Rebecca Burlend lived with the Yelliotts and died aged, respectively, 87 and 77 years.

In the book it is mentioned that after coming to this country, the author had twins. If there is anything in heredity, it may be noted that the Yelliotts had two pair of twins. Another child of the Burlends was Sarah Allen, whose daughter married Sylvester Thompson. Sarah lived near Detroit and Thompson lived near Pittsfield at the time the History of Pike County was printed.

Daniel Burns, who formerly lived near Big Blue in Detroit tp., or one of his ancestors, may have been the Burns mentioned in the book as a neighbor of the author. It may be possible to definitely establish the identity of the author from the records of the real estate purchases of the husband of the pioneer author. He first bought eighty acres from a man named Oakes, which was registered in Quincy in November, 1831. That may have been the eighty that extended to the south line of Flint tp. and was later owned by William Burlend. Afterwards the husband of the author purchased a larger tract nearby from Mr. Paddock. This, she says, had been registered at the Land Office in Pittsfield. Later a man named Carr wrongfully preempted the same piece and registered it at Quincy, Illinois. This piece may have been the tract standing on the north line of Detroit tp. and later owned by William Burlend.

If the old record books are still in existence, they will probably settle the question of authorship, but if not, information may be obtained from the Yelliott descendants, or perhaps Mr. Jack Murphy, of Detroit, may know something about it. If you are interested and do discover the name of the author, it would be well to advise the British Museum and the Library of Congress so they can enter it on their lists.

Yours very truly,

OLIVER R. BARRETT

Publishers' Preface

Mr. Guy Littell,
350 East Cermak Road,
Chicago, Illinois.

Dear Guy:

I think you may safely enter the name of the author in your copy of "A True Picture of Emigration," etc., as Rebecca Burlend.

I sifted the facts from the book that might indicate the identity of the author and I searched the histories and atlases of Pike County and came to the conclusion that Rebecca Burlend was the author. I thereupon wrote Jess M. Thompson, of Pittsfield, Illinois, and suggested that he pursue the investigation and verify it if possible. Curiously enough, Mr. Thompson happened to be the great grandson of the author of the book. Mr. Thompson wrote me as follows:

"Dear Mr. Barrett:

I have a letter here which reached me at the time when I was having a siege of flu, and which, it appears, has not been answered—a letter which, by the way, I read with a great deal of interest.

The little volume to which you refer, which was published anonymously in London, was, as you guessed, the recorded experiences here in the New World of my maternal great-grandmother, Rebecca Burlend, who with her husband, John Burlend, and their five children, landed at Phillips Ferry in the year 1831, after a long

Publishers' Preface

and harrowing trip from Yorkshire to New Orleans, and thence up the Mississippi and Illinois rivers.

Her son, Edward Burlend, who remained in England, was a schoolmaster and the author of several volumes of both prose and poetry. His most important contribution to Yorkshire literature was the novel 'Amy Thornton.'

Rebecca Burlend's daughter, Sarah Allen, was my grandmother. Her daughter, Charlotte, married Sylvester Thompson, they being my parents."

All of which goes to show that investigation of literary problems is not only extremely interesting as a diversion but sometimes brings results.

Yours very truly,

OLIVER R. BARRETT

While this bit of early western history lacks the dramatic character of many of its predecessors, it depicts the same spirit of courage and self-reliance that permeates them all.

THE PUBLISHERS

Christmas, 1936.

Contents

PAGE

PUBLISHER'S PREFACE v

HISTORICAL INTRODUCTION xvii

REPRODUCTION OF THE ORIGINAL

   TITLE PAGE 3

PREFATORY REMARKS 5

CHAPTER 1 7

CHAPTER 2 15

CHAPTER 3 33

CHAPTER 4 58

CHAPTER 5 89

INDEX 161

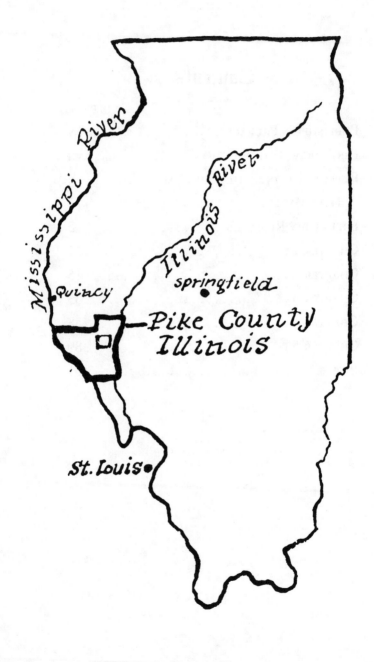

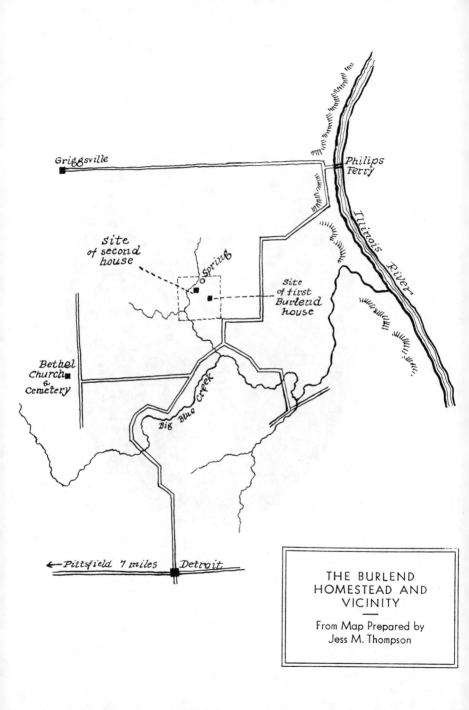

Griggsville

Philips Ferry

Illinois River

site
of second
house

Spring

site
of first
Burlend
house

Bethel
Church
&
Cemetery

Big Blue Creek

←Pittsfield 7 miles   Detroit

THE BURLEND
HOMESTEAD AND
VICINITY
—
From Map Prepared by
Jess M. Thompson

JOHN BURLEND

Historical Introduction

PUBLICATION of *The Lakeside Classics* was begun in 1903, and the current volume (number thirty-four in the series) is the twenty-first prepared by the present Editor. Since 1911, the annual volumes have been devoted to the field of western history, and with but two exceptions the narratives reprinted have been written by men. The reason for this masculine preponderance is obvious. The careers of women commonly afford but little material for the pen of the biographer, and comparatively seldom do women themselves undertake to record their life-stories.

The two narratives by feminine authors we have published hitherto are Mrs. Christiana Tillson's *A Woman's Story of Pioneer Illinois*, issued in 1919, and Mrs. Juliette A. Kinzie's *Wau-Bun, The "Early Day" in the North-West*, issued in 1932. Both authors were unusual women, and their narratives are among the finest in the entire series of *The Lakeside Classics*. Both were women of New England birth and breeding who came as brides to the region west of Lake Michigan.

Here the parallel ends, however, for Mrs.
Kinzie's highly individual story deals with
the world of the red man and the fur trader,
while Mrs. Tillson's story is the more common one of the pioneer life of an American
woman settler in the West.

The narrative of Rebecca Burlend, now
presented to the reader, differs in certain
marked respects from both the Tillson and
the Kinzie recitals. Compared with Mrs.
Burlend, the other women occupied a dis-
tinctly higher station in life. Both were New
England gentlewomen, and both were city
dwellers who moved in the best society of
their time and place. Rebecca Burlend, on
the contrary, sprang from the peasantry of
rural Yorkshire, and from infancy was inured
to a life of toil and hardship. She came to
America, as millions of others have done, to
improve her material lot in life. In this, she
succeeded, ultimately, although the present-
day reader of her narrative may perhaps
wonder whether the result was worth the
effort expended in achieving it. In America,
as in England, she remained the hard-working wife of a hard-worked farmer. Only in
the evening of her days did she enjoy the
leisure which comes with assured prosperity;
and only through the chance possession of a
son imbued with literary talent and training

did she succeed in recording her story for posterity, instead of becoming merely one of the unsung millions of nineteenth-century immigrants to America.

Mrs. Burlend's narrative was written primarily for the information of people of her own class in England who might be weighing the question of migration to America. For their benefit, she related the story of her own prior experience in this respect. It is clear that she was a woman of more than ordinary will power and native force of character. She tells her story simply, and as truthfully, probably, as any recital of one's own experiences can be told. Between the Burlends (and their followers) of a century ago and the Matanuska emigrants of current memory lies a wide gulf. The emigrants of 1935, spoon-fed at every step in their progress by the agents of an all-compassionate government, would have understood as little the native resourcefulness of those of 1831, as the latter would have comprehended the lot of the present-day emigrants. Whether the emigrants of 1831 or those of 1935 will prove more fortunate in the long run, must remain for the future to disclose.

Mrs. Burlend's story begins with the reasons for the New-World migration in the summer of 1831, and continues until success in the momentous venture of transplanting the family to a distant and alien wilderness had been achieved. We have here the task of supplying the reader with such additional pertinent information as will aid in promoting his appreciation of the story she presents. Rebecca Burton was born in Yorkshire, of humble parentage, May 18, 1793. Although we lack the date of her marriage to John Burlend, it must have been at a comparatively early age, for Edward, the eldest son, was a schoolteacher when the migration to America in 1831, took place. The hard circumstances of her married life in England are briefly hinted at in the opening pages of her narrative. Further light on this point is afforded by the statements concerning the life of Edward Burlend. In his *Village Rhymes*, a book of poems published in 1858, he states that the poems were chiefly composed in periods of illness: "Brought up at the plough till I was eighteen years of age, and then thrown upon my own resources, to make my way as a teacher, it will be easily understood that for many years I had to devote my leisure time to strictly laborious study."

Edward Burlend spent his mature life as a schoolmaster in his native Yorkshire, dying at Swillington, April 6, 1875. His tombstone inscription in Swillington Churchyard recites that "under many social disadvantages, and under extreme delicacy of constitution, he taught, with marked success, a competent knowledge of the classics, mathematics, and other branches of science and literature. As an original thinker, his prose works, and as an elegant writer, his poetry, will long remain evidences of his powers and ability. Courteous, peaceful, and retiring, he lived respected to his end, truly deserving the character of a 'just man'."

Tombstone inscriptions are ever kind, and the writer of Edward's obituary may not have been a competent critic of his literary output. The great Library of Congress contains none of his writings, and its bibliographer reports that an "extensive search" of English book catalogs, dictionaries of authors, and Yorkshire local histories discloses no evidence either of his writings or of his existence. Perhaps this report merely indicates anew the fleeting character of all earthly fame. The British Museum catalog lists two of Edward Burlend's books, one, *A Catechism of English History*, published at London in 1855, and another, *Amy Thornton; or the Curate's Daughter*, published at London and Leeds in 1862. Jess M. Thompson of Pittsfield, Illinois, possesses a copy of his book of poems, a

small volume of about 200 pages, whose
title page, for bibliographical reasons, we
copy in full: *"Village Rhymes; or Poems on
Various Subjects, Principally Appertaining
to Incidents in Village Life*. By Edward
Burlend. Leeds, Printed by David Green,
Boar-Lane, 1858." To say that the poems
are Mid-Victorian in character would be
trite and meaningless. Through them runs
a recurrent vein of melancholy, whose cause
is perhaps adequately suggested by the tombstone obituary of the author, which we have
already quoted.

To complete the roll of Edward Burlend's
literary output, we must add to the foregoing
his rendition of his mother's American narrative, which quite probably became the most
important of all his publications. Although
Rebecca Burlend was not illiterate, it is obvious that she could scarcely have put her
story into the finished literary form in which
it appears in print. Although the narrative
is undoubtedly the story of Rebecca, the
form in which it is cast is equally undoubtedly the handiwork of her schoolmaster-poet
son, Edward. He proved a capable editor,
and produced a faithful factual narrative,
in the main; but the precise language, and
some of the reflections embodied in it (for
example, the comment, in the concluding

pages, upon the causes of England's greatness) are the product of Edward Burlend's brain and pen. In short, mother and son stand as co-authors of the narrative. The mother related her story to her son; and the latter transformed it into the book, which was published at London in the summer of 1848 as a paper-bound pamphlet of 62 pages, entitled *A True Picture of Emigration: Or Fourteen Years in the Interior of North America; Being a Full and Impartial Account of the Various Difficulties and Ultimate Success of an English Family Who Emigrated from Barwick-In-Elmet, Near Leeds, in the Year 1831.*

For some reason, the pamphlet was issued anonymously (perhaps the intimacy of the story caused the authors to shrink from disclosing their identity), thereby entailing upon future American bibliographers and historians a considerable burden of trouble. Prof. S. J. Buck in his fine Illinois bibliography of *Travel and Description 1765–1865* (*Illinois Historical Collections*, Vol. IX) published in 1914, affords no indication of the identity of the authors, and the bibliographers of the Library of Congress have been likewise ignorant concerning it until the present day. But to Jess M. Thompson of Pittsfield, Illinois, a descendant of Rebecca

Burlend, as well as to other descendants (and their neighbors) the identity of the authors has never been a secret. Herein, for the first time in print, the story is told, based upon information chiefly supplied the present Editor by Mr. Thompson.

The struggle for economic security so valiantly waged by John and Rebecca Burlend met with its appropriate reward. By 1846, when Rebecca made the visit to her former English home which is described in the closing pages of her narrative, the objective forevisioned a decade and a half earlier had been achieved. From the despairing, beaten, tenant family which fled from Yorkshire in 1831, the Burlends had become transformed into the confident possessors in fee simple of an extensive acreage in an agricultural region as fine as any in America. Already they were landlords, receiving the rental from their surplus acres, while around them were their children, the elder ones already arrived at manhood's estate.

Under the circumstances, Rebecca's visit home must have been for her a proud and gratifying occasion. How eagerly her old neighbors listened to her recital of her experiences in the far-away world of Pike County, Illinois, can best be understood by those readers who have themselves known lives of toil and poverty, and the incessant seeking for an escape into a securer and more gracious condition. The Editor has found no contemporary record of the date of this return journey, and the dates supplied by descendants, based on family tradition and belief, are conflicting. The evidence supplied by the concluding pages of the narrative itself seems to establish the year, with a high degree of probability, as 1846. Probably this detail could be certainly established, if adequate time to investigate it were available, but circumstances beyond the Editor's control have denied him the opportunity of pursuing the matter further.

By rare good fortune, however, almost in the closing hours of the preparation of the volume for the printer, contact was established with Miss Hazel Whalen of Chicago, a great-granddaughter of John and Rebecca Burlend, who supplemented most usefully the information already supplied by Jess M. Thompson concerning a second edition of the Burlend family saga. Mr. Thompson himself has never seen this edition, but James Farrand of Griggsville, who visited England many years ago, relates that he somewhere saw a copy, and that it contained the names of a number of families who had migrated to Pike County in consequence

of Mrs. Burlend's visit home and of the publication of her story in 1848. Miss Whalen
relates that about four years ago she saw,
and had temporary possession of a copy,
whose owner desires to remain unknown.
Miss Whalen, however, copied certain data,
which disclose some interesting facts. The
new edition was issued either in 1856 or
1857 (both dates being given) with a complete change of title, and with Edward
Burlend's name as the author. On the fly-
leaf appears "*The Wesleyan Emigrants,* by
Edward Burlend (London. Longman, Brown,
Green, and Longman; Simpkin, Marshall,
and Co. 1857)." On the title-page proper,
with the same publishers but with the date
1856 instead of 1857, is this amplified title:

Wesleyan Christianity
Tested and Exemplified
being an
Authentic Narrative
of
Striking Events in the
History of a Wesleyan Family
of Yorkshire Emigrants
in the Back Woods of America
by
Edward Burlend

Historical Introduction

The foreword to the edition stated that the book had first been published in 1848, and that over 2000 copies had been sold in the city of Leeds alone. Because of this demand, the second edition was being published. The lay reader will perhaps marvel that a narrative which aroused such widespread interest, and which affected so deeply the lives of a number of English families, should prove so difficult to trace at the present time. The historian, however, sadly familiar with the neglect and oblivion which sooner or later overtakes all ordinary records, will feel gratified, rather, over the fact that a number of American libraries have copies of the first edition, which now obtains renewed publicity and distribution by being included in *The Lakeside Classics*.

The reader will observe, in the concluding "Note" to the narrative, the statement by Edward Burlend that several families had already departed for America, moved by Rebecca Burlend's recital of her experiences there. Still others followed, finding homes in Pike County, where their descendants are still numerously represented. Bethel Cemetery, a beautiful country churchyard, is chiefly populated by these English families. Here John and Rebecca Burlend rest from their labors, in the midst of relatives and neighbors for whose presence in America they were directly responsible. The present church, erected over half a century ago, replaces an earlier structure on the same site. Two or three miles away across the lush and fertile Illinois River Valley lies the site of the Burlend homestead. To the simple House of God Rebecca was wont to trudge across the intervening fields, carrying her shoes and stockings in her hand, to be donned, upon arrival, before entering the church.

The loghouse which became the first home of the Burlends in America stood "in the center" of the northeast quarter of the northeast quarter of section 6, Detroit Township, about three miles north of Detroit village, and about the same distance southwest of Valley City. The cabin stood on a hillside, overlooking the adjacent level valley, and distant but a few rods from a beautiful spring, whose delicious water still pours forth from the rocky slope. The presence of this spring no doubt determined the location of the cabin by Squatter Oakes, who built it. When the Burlends arrived at a state of prosperity sufficient to permit the erection of a better home, they located it on the same hill-slope, a few rods farther away from the spring. Both cabins have long since vanished from earth, and the casual passer-by would be unlikely to observe any trace of their former existence. Mr. Francis Allen of Pittsfield, octogenarian grandson of Rebecca Burlend, remembers the second cabin, and in August, 1936, he and Jess M. Thompson of Pittsfield conducted the writer to the farm and identified the now-forgotten homesites.

Upon returning to America from her visit to England in 1846, Rebecca Burlend was accompanied to her Pike County home by her daughter (now Mary Yelliott) and her family. The Yelliotts located near the parental homestead, and in their declining years John and Rebecca Burlend found a safe haven with them. To the end of her life Rebecca remained the plain, sturdy woman whose character is so clearly depicted in her narrative—thrifty, hard-working, God-fearing. Her still-surviving grandchild, Francis Allen of Pittsfield, describes her as possessed of a pleasant disposition. She never complained of her hardships; instead, when speaking of early times she would say that although hard, they always managed to get along. In England she had learned something of herbs and homely medical lore, and in Pike County she served for years, without money or other price, as the neighborhood

physician. Mr. Albert Rhodes of Griggsville, now an aged man, relates that when-
ever anyone became ill, the family would
send for her. She found great solace in her
pipe, and in the years of her retirement from
active labor she spent much of her time
smoking before the Yelliott fireplace. Francis Allen still possesses her favorite chair,
whose rockers were worn out by the often-
repeated process of drawing it forward to
light her pipe from the coals and then slid-
ing it back again to a comfortable position.
Her old-age likeness may be seen in the
portrait published in the present volume.
Jess Thompson's mother, who died in 1933,
related that Rebecca (her grandmother)
was slight in figure, and had a command-
ing expression. Francis Allen, on the contrary, remembers her as a fairly tall and
fairly heavy woman. He also recalls John
Burlend as a tall, heavy man, fond of prac-
tical jokes, and popular with the boys and
young men. He died, April 9, 1871, in
his eighty-eighth year. Rebecca survived
but a few months longer, dying January
31, 1872. Four decades of life in the New-
World home had been granted them, but
the significant portion of the period lies
in the fifteen years which the narrative
covers.

Historical Introduction

The passage of a century has wrought many changes in America's national problems. In recent decades the welcome formerly extended to aliens has been sharply curtailed, and no longer do we offer asylum to ambitious and discontented men and women from all the earth. However wise, or necessary, the present national policy may be, it seems clear that the Burlends and their Yorkshire neighbors who came to Pike County a century ago made a distinct contribution to the commonwealth of their adoption. To them and their children pioneer Illinois offered a new opportunity in life. They embraced it eagerly, and in doing so became numbered among the builders of civilization in the region where they elected to settle. Happy the commonwealth which gains such immigrants; happy the settlers who found such an entrancing New-World home.

M. M. QUAIFE

Detroit Public Library
Sept. 15, 1936

A True Picture of
Emigration

A TRUE PICTURE

OF

EMIGRATION :

OR FOURTEEN YEARS IN

THE INTERIOR OF NORTH AMERICA;

BEING A FULL AND IMPARTIAL ACCOUNT
OF THE VARIOUS DIFFICULTIES AND ULTIMATE SUCCESS
OF AN ENGLISH FAMILY

WHO EMIGRATED FROM BARWICK-IN-ELMET,

NEAR LEEDS, IN THE YEAR 1831.

———

LONDON:

PUBLISHED BY G. BERGER, HOLYWELL-STREET;

LEEDS: DAVID GREEN: MANCHESTER: A. HEYWOOD;
AND ALL OTHER BOOKSELLERS.

Prefatory Remarks

—

IN submitting the contents of this volume to the notice of the public, the writer begs to state that the materials and facts herein contained were delivered to him *viva voce* by his mother, the principal agent in the narrative, during a late visit to this, her native country.

To him the account seemed interesting in the highest degree, an opinion in which such of his friends as have perused the manuscript have invariably concurred.

The present state of the public mind in regard to emigration has suggested the propriety of immediately giving publicity to the narrative, which is what might be termed the Diary of a Yorkshire Emigrant in the United States of America.

How far such a production is required the public will now determine. It is what it professes to be: 'a true picture;' the incidents are facts—not fiction; the language only in which they are described belongs to the author.

Swillington, August 1st, 1848.

EDWARD BURLEND

A True Picture of
Emigration

Chapter 1

WHATEVER may have been our success in America, I can attribute but little of it to myself; as I gave up the idea of ending my days in my own country with the utmost reluctance, and should never have become an emigrant, if obedience to ✓ my husband's wishes had left me any alternative. His motives, briefly stated, were these:—In the year 1817 we took a small farm at a village in Yorkshire on a lease for fourteen years, and as corn was at that time selling well, the rent was fixed at too high a rate for us to obtain a comfortable livelihood. We did indeed by dint of great industry and strict economy, maintain our credit to the end of the lease; but the severe struggles we had to endure to meet our payments, the gradual diminution of our little property, and the entire absence of any prospects of being able to supply the wants of a large family had tended effectually to fix my husband's purpose of trying what could be done in the western world. We accordingly disposed of our little furniture, settled our pecuniary affairs, and ultimately began our long journey the last week in August 1831.

The reader will now enquire to what part of America we were going, or whether we had any plans as to the locality of our future home. This is an important consideration for every emigrant, though little attended to by many. We were not, however, like the poor Northumbrian, who, on landing at New York a few years ago, required a person whom he met in the street, to direct him to the back settlements. My husband had travelled many miles to obtain a sight of private American letters, and after maturely considering all the intelligence he could collect, he determined to go to Pike County, Illinois, to a person named Mr. B—, who had settled there a year or two before, and written to a brother of his in this country.[1]

[1]Charles Bickerdike, the first of his name to settle in Pike County, came to America (and Illinois) and settled in Flint Township, Pike County, about 1828. It was the reading of his letters to his brother in England which determined the migration of the Burlends. The Bickerdike family is still represented in Pike County, and the graves of earlier members of the line may be seen in Bethel Cemetery where Rebecca Burlend

A True Picture of Emigration

Without further preface, we are therefore to be considered on our way from the centre of Yorkshire to Liverpool, self, husband, and five children, the eldest a boy about nine years old, two others we were leaving behind, the one my eldest son engaged as an under teacher in a boarding school, the other my eldest daughter serving also in a respectable family.[1] To persons such as we were, who had never been forty miles from home, a journey by waggon and railway, where every hour presents the eye with something new, does not afford the best opportunity for

and her husband lie buried. Charles Bickerdike is also buried in Bethel Cemetery, according to family information, although no monument identifies his grave.

[1] The author and her husband had fourteen children in all. Four had died in England before the migration to America, and two more (Edward, the "eldest son" and Mary, the "eldest daughter" of the present sentence) remained behind. The five children who shared in the family migration were John, then nine years old, Hannah, eight years old, Sarah, three years old, Charlotte, and William, an infant. John served in the Mexican War and was slain in a soldiers' brawl while returning to his Illinois home. Hannah married Thomas Dalby and lived to her ninetieth year, dying at Griggsville in 1913. Sarah married Francis Allen, and Charlotte married Daniel Burns. William, the infant of 1831, died at Griggsville in 1900. Information taken from article by Jess M. Thompson in *Pike County Republican* (Pittsfield), July 22, 1936.

reflection; we in consequence reached Liverpool before we fully felt the importance of the step we were taking. Nature had indeed yielded a little as we gazed upon the scenes of our industry, which time had endeared, for the last time. But it was at Liverpool, when we had got our luggage to a boarding-house and were waiting the departure of a vessel, that the throes of leaving England and all its endearments put our courage to a test the most severe. Our minds were now undisturbed by surrounding objects; we occupied a small apartment for which we paid two shillings a day, without even the indulgence of a fire to cook our provisions. The dark smoky walls of the opposite buildings were the only prospect that the situation of our sojourn could afford. Predisposed to melancholy as we were, no one can be surprised when he is told that its effects were soon apparent. A stranger would have thought us a most unsocial family, as we sat in profound silence for an hour together, only now and then a sigh would escape us tending to vary but not to enliven this painful monotony. Even our children participated in our disquietude, and seemed to lose their wonted vivacity. My dear husband, who before had displayed nothing but hardihood, on this occasion had almost played the

woman. After a deep silence I not unfre-
quently observed his eyes suffused with ✓
tears, which though unnoticed by him, fell
in quick succession down his sunbrowned
cheeks. We were six days in this abode, and
I may venture to assert that he did not spend
six hours of the time in the forgetfulness of
sleep.

At last the day dawned on which we were
to embark. We had already bespoke our
berths and paid a deposit to secure them.
It was a critical period: my husband ap- ✓
peared to feel as if all the responsibility was
laid upon him. He doubtless felt for himself; but his children and myself were the
principal objects of his solicitude. Those he
was leaving behind would be left to the wide
world without any one to watch over them;
and that at a time when the passions which
actuate the human breast, are in the greatest need of parental authority and advice.
The destiny of those he was taking with him
appeared about to be consigned to a vague
uncertain probability. The die was going to
be cast. In twelve hours more we should be
on the deep, where return would be impracticable. These considerations,—the perils of
the sea the more dreaded because unknown,
together with many other weighty considerations which a father and a husband in such a

situation could not but feel, got the better of his natural prowess, and that morning he addressed me in the following manner: "O Rebecca, I cannot do it, I cannot do it! for myself I fear nothing; but the impenetrable gloom and uncertainty attending this step completely bewilders me. Should anything befall me, what will become of you and my children on the stormy ocean, or in a strange land and among pathless woods. Bad as our prospects are in England we must go back! Such another night as the last has been I cannot survive! this terrible suspense and anxiety tears me in pieces."

Sentiments like these a few months ago would have been hailed with delight, and even then I must confess I felt a sort of inward satisfaction, although I knew them to be rather the effects of his feelings than his mental decisions. If we returned I knew he could not be satisfied with his condition, still less with his present conduct. I however acquiesced in silence, only replying, I would do what he thought best. We accordingly began to remove our boxes back to the luggage waggon, whither I accompanied him; but all the time we were thus employed he appeared like one whose movements are coerced. The smile with which he usually accompanied his addresses no longer appeared. I saw it would not do; we returned to our children like those who return from the interment of a near relative, in mournful silence. Never before had I felt so much to devolve on me, √ and perhaps never in my life did I so much feel it my duty to practise self-denial. My native land was as dear to me as ever: my two children, to whom I had bidden adieu, were strong ties. But the consciousness that it was my duty to bear up the sinking spirits of my partner, left me only one course to adopt. For a moment I raised my eyes to him "who sitteth above the water-floods," and with feelings I am not able to depict, broke silence as follows;—

"I admit, my dear husband, that our situation is a very trying one; but remember how often and how long you have resolved to go to America; hitherto we have experienced nothing that we did not anticipate; and should any calamity befall us on our journey, you have adopted emigration only from a conviction that it would tend to the good of the family; and the Almighty is as able to preserve us and our children across the seas or in America as he is in England. Besides, if we return, we have broken up our home and sold our furniture, and should be worse situated than ever; let us even go, and look to Providence for success." The above advice on my part operated like a charm. All that has been said of the effects of martial music was here realized. His answer was rather in deed than in word. In two hours more our luggage was removed from the waggon, where it had just been placed with a view of returning home, to the ship in which we had taken our berths. The remainder of the day till four o'clock was spent in procuring stores, cooking utensils, &c., necessary for our voyage; and when the sun went down on the second of September, 1831, we were on the waters; having previously confided ourselves to the care of Him "whom earth and seas are ready to obey."

Chapter 2

AFTER we had thus finally determined and put it out of our power to alter that decision, our minds were more at ease than before. There being no longer any doubt as to whether we should go to America, the suspense which had hitherto been so afflicting began in a great measure to subside. My husband resumed his wonted cheerfulness, and expressed his belief that the course we had ultimately adopted would prove the best in the end. We were now passengers, in the steerage, on the vessel "*Home*," bound for New Orleans. Our reasons for sailing to that port the most distant in North America, and not in a direct course to the Illinois, were on account of the ready transit we should make thence into the interior up the Mississippi; whereas, by landing at New York, Boston, or Philadelphia, we should have had to cross the Alleghany mountains, and travel a great distance by land, which would have been both very troublesome on account of our luggage, and very expensive.

The perplexed state of mind in which we were prior to embarking had prevented our noticing or enjoying the fine sights which the port of Liverpool presents. I speak not of the magnitude of the town, nor of its architectural decorations, but of the immense forests of ships, which on every hand strike the eye of the beholder as he sails out of the harbour. Whatever might have been my ideas of the greatness and wealth of England before, I am sure they were greatly enlarged when I beheld for the first time in my life those unwieldly instruments of commerce crowded like forest trees on the sea further than the eye could reach. As the wind was favourable we soon lost sight of the shore. Yet the eye with unwearied vigilance kept steadily fixed on the few eminences which remained visible, till they gradually waned into obscurity, and at last disappeared altogether. The reader may think me needlessly precise in naming this circumstance; but I assure him there were many on board, who, as well as myself, felt a gratification in gazing at the naked rocks that projected from the land that had given us birth; and when it was finally announced that England was no longer visible, there was not a person in the ship who would not have heartily responded amen to the prayer, 'God bless it.' For myself, I felt as if I was leaving all I had been wont to prize; and when I could no longer see the shore, I shall never forget how enviously I looked upon the vessels that were approaching the shores I was leaving. I followed them with my eye, one by one, till quite weary with looking I descended into the cabin, and endeavoured to be reconciled to my situation by exercising myself in some necessary employment.

Although we were entire strangers to a sea-faring life, we found we had been judicious in the choice of our provisions: we were well supplied with oatmeal and flour, bacon, biscuits, tea and coffee, &c., and as we had to cook for ourselves at a fire which supplied all the steerage passengers, I found I should have something to do besides descrying distant sails, and sighing a blessing to those bound for England.

At home I had always been fond of regularity with regard to the dinner hour, but I soon found if I continued my punctual habits on board I should often be liable to be laughed at for my pains, and lose my dinner in the bargain. Imagine to yourself, kind reader, a small fire surrounded by half-a-dozen sturdy rustics, as busy boiling, roasting, and frying, as if their lives depended upon a single meal, and I will hazard an opinion you would be very hungry before you would venture among them. I do not say they would eat

17

you; but either from the motion of the ship, or their uncouthness, your fortune would be better than mine if you got your meal prepared without being scalded. For the above reasons I soon forgot my punctuality, and through the remainder of the voyage our custom was to cook and eat when we could, for seasons are not unknown on ship-board when both must be dispensed with.

During the first few days the weather was calm: we had sailed down the Irish channel before the much dreaded sea-sickness began to annoy us. I had even begun to think, that like many other evils, its terrors had been overrated; but before we had been a week on board a heavy gale began to blow from the north-west, the sky became dark and unsettled, when I began to be exceedingly sick; a disorder in which nearly all the passengers participated. Painfully afflictive as this malady was, it soon became of little consideration on account of a more alarming misfortune which threatened to befall us. The sea was beginning to be unusually rough, its huge foaming waves came dashing against the sides of the vessel, as if they had been let loose to destroy it. Sometimes we appeared about to leave the waters, and become inhabitants of ærial regions; then again one might suppose the ship was instantaneously descending into the caverns of the deep, overwhelmed by the mass of waters which on all sides encompassed it, and at times came sweeping over the deck with irresistible fury. A thousand times I thought the ship would be upset by the force of the tempest, which, roaring tremendously, carried all before it, and often laid our masts nearly level with the main; when suddenly regaining her upright position, she seemed to be contending with the blast, and by a movement I can scarcely account for, obtruding her briny sails against the forces of the storm. The crew were all in action; their shoutings were vociferous;—louder even than the voice of the wind. Terror and dismay were on every hand. The captain alone preserved his serenity; his orders were delivered in a loud but unfaultering tone; he might have been a divinity of the waters so dignified and majestic was his deportment on this occasion. Not so the passengers,— they were indeed mortals, and suppliants too. Impiety was banished from the ship. You might have seen those, who yesterday could not conclude a sentence without the usual flourish of an oath, now on their knees serious enough. The night came on,—the passengers were ordered below: such a night I never witnessed. The storm was incessant.

A True Picture of Emigration

The timbers creaked alarmingly; and the sailors, hurrying to and fro on the deck, filled us with renewed consternation. Every moment we expected the waters to rush in upon us. I shall never forget the horrors of that night, increased as they were by the heart-rending moanings of my despairing companions. It was not the time for reflection: reason had little control over our actions; as our fears directed, so we conducted ourselves. Nature's bonds, however, were not entirely dissevered, for then even I found myself in a corner of the cabin, my husband at my right hand, which he often clasped in his, and our dear little children huddled around us, giving us their little hands to fondle over and caress. Art thou a mother, gentle reader, thou mayest in part conceive what my feelings were; but there are sensations which no description can embody; there are emotions which nothing but experience can explain: of this kind were mine.

At length the morning began to dawn; we were all anxiety to see the day, and ascertain our real situation. Of all the emotions of which the human bosom is susceptible, suspense is the most intolerable. We desired to know the worst; but our orders were to keep within, and we feared to disobey. The little light we obtained from the semipellucid glass at the top of our cabin, was of no avail. Our ears had caused us to think the storm was abating; but this only increased our anxiety, as we were afraid to hope, lest we should be deceived, when to our surprise the cabin door sprung open; it was the captain himself who had opened it. His appearance was like one of those celestial visitors, which the sacred pages have pourtrayed on errands of mercy. We hurried to meet him; but he desired us to be at ease, assuring us the danger was past. His expressive words "the danger is past," were repeated again and again through all the cabin; and now the scene was changed. In the place of lamentations and the voice of despair, were immediately heard jocularity and the tumult of mirth. His words had metamorphosed the room. Forgotten or disregarded were all the pious vows which had been made the preceding night. "They ate and they drank and they rose up to play;" but few could be seen in the attitude of praise. The storm had indeed abated; and, such is human nature, religion had vanished at the same time. The following day I learnt we had been driven considerably out of our course into the Bay of Biscay; but no further injury was sustained except a little to the cordage, which the sailors shortly put right, and before evening the sails were again unfurled, and our ship in good repair, majestically making head-way across the Atlantic. This was the only storm we encountered during our passage; it was a severe one; even the sailors spoke of it with concern, and seemed aware our danger had been great.

A long sea-voyage is generally allowed to be a tedious time, and there is some foundation for the remark, when it is considered how little variety is there observable. The ship, your companions, the sky above you and the 'dark blue ocean' below, with occasionally a solitary sail gliding quietly along at a distance, constitute the principal objects that come under the notice of ordinary travellers. There is nothing of that everlasting newness and beauty,—that pleasing variety of hill and dale, of trees whose foliage is varied by a thousand hues, meandering streams, village towers and spires that everywhere meet the eye in an English landscape. Nor is the ear more favoured than the eye. The creaking of the cables and the mast, the coarse discordant notes of the seamen and the monotonous dashing of the waves against the vessel, are the most common and almost the entire sounds that a sea-breeze can boast. The melodious warbling of the grove are there unknown; and when the night-dews are falling, the mellow flute notes of

the swain breathing innocence and love,
never once remind the passenger on the deep
that the labours of the day are ended, and
the star of evening appears.

The sea, nevertheless, has its beauties and
grandeur; but these are rather perceptible to
the reflecting mind than the external sense.
One evening I well remember when we were
about half-way across the Atlantic, I was
alone on the deck, pensively considering the
peculiarity of my situation, and impatiently
desirous to know what my future condition
should be, when casting my eyes towards
the east I beheld a most magnificent spec-
tacle: the large full moon was just clearing
the watery horizon. I always love to see the
moon beginning her nocturnal rambles; her
beams are the light in which meditation appears the most lovely; but when on that delightful evening, in the midst of the great
Atlantic, I beheld the same kind planet,
beneath whose balmy light I had gamboled
in my childhood and conversed on subjects
the most endearing in maturer age, my whole
soul was overpowered with ecstacy. Bear
with me, kind reader, bear with a woman's
weakness, if I tell thee I looked upon her as
an old companion, and addressed her as a
bosom friend, so forcibly did she remind me
of the many delightful and happy hours I

had spent under her auspicious beams in my native land. Independent of these interesting associations, her appearance at such a time and in such a place was highly imposing, and calculated in a remarkable degree to remind me of the insignificance of man and his noblest performances. Impressed in this manner I gazed upon her broad disk, and O how magnificently splendid! I next surveyed the deep, gilded on one side by her rays and on the other terminating the view by a dark half-visible horizon; and what a world of water seemed to surround me. I then considered the ship,—poor feeble bark, thought I, how insecure thou art! a single wave could undo thee. Lastly I looked at myself: the contrast was sickening; human pride could not bear it; I cast my eyes once more upon the moon, and returned into the cabin.

To proceed,—by the time we had well got half-way across the water, our impatience to see land daily increased; the hours began to pass more tardily along than before. Those that kept their minds most engaged were the most happy; a piece of philosophy this which will generally hold true. I am not going to describe my fellow-passengers as philosophers, the few traits I have already given prove they were not; but to do them justice, many of them were expert hands at dispelling melancholy. This they did sometimes by cracking jokes at each other, sometimes by relating portions of their histories, or celebrating the matchless heroism or strength of their kindred. Thus by degrees having severally acquired an epitome of each other's lives, a sort of community was formed and neighbourhoods established, less regulated indeed by locality than peculiar likings. When first we set out each must cook for himself, or at most for his own family; now you might have seen three or four messing together, having previously agreed to throw their respective provisions into one common store. By this means there were fewer dishes to prepare, and consequently better accommodation. We were too strict economists to adopt the joining system; and our solicitude respecting our journey caused us rather to avoid intimacy with our companions than to court it. Yes, many a time when mirth and noise have been the prevailing order on deck, have I sought retirement to muse upon the past, and pry into the future. I own such conduct was unwise; I should have been happier if I could have mingled in the diversions of my companions: but, reader, knowest thou not when the heart is sick the very means which should be beneficial are often the most repulsive?

A True Picture of Emigration

It was impossible, from the nature of things, that I could be happy, while as yet we were travelling we scarcely knew whither. On one occasion while thus alone on the deck, near the cook's cabin, I perceived an unusual quantity of smoke issuing from the door and chimney, and on looking down I perceived a person named Jack, who by the by had stolen on board at Liverpool and was working his passage, involved in a cloud of smoke and flame from a pan of pitch, which by accident he had spilled into the fire. I gave the alarm, and all hands were immediately on the spot. The wood was beginning to ignite, and if it had not been attended to with the utmost promptitude our situation would soon have been awful. A mattress, which happened to be near, was instantly put upon the chimney to prevent the draught, and buckets of water were plentifully thrown in at the door, so that in a very short time the fire was extinguished. Poor Jack fared the worst: his right arm was almost roasted, which caused him to be, as an invalid, exempt from duty to the end of the voyage. His misfortune excited the compassion of many on board, some of whom presented him with wearing apparel, &c., of which he was in great need. For myself by being in the centre of the crowd, I became entangled in a rope near the mouth of the cabin, which subjected me to the stench and steam thence arising. I was however soon released from my accidental fetters, and laden with the grateful acknowledgments of all around.

Another time while pacing upon the deck, I was almost struck dumb to see my son, the boy before alluded to, a fine youth, but uncommonly daring,[1] fast asleep on the bowsprit. The least accidental movement and he would have lost his equilibrium, and been precipitated into the water. Alarmed as I was, I did all that a mother could do in such a situation to preserve the life of one so dear. My husband was just at hand. I made no noise, but all in agitation pointed out the cause of my distress. He soon understood me,—and, with all the concern of an affectionate father, hastened softly towards the lad, and rescued him from that imminent peril into which his daring spirit had unwittingly led him.

The recital of these incidents brings me, through the order in which they occurred, towards the West Indies; and to another occurrence which for a short time caused a greater alarm than any thing we met with during the voyage. The circumstances are

[1]The venturesome character of John Burlend, the child here alluded to, is still a matter of family tradition. Information supplied by Jess M. Thompson.

as fresh in my mind as if they had transpired only yesterday. I had been observing with interest and pity a number of flying fishes occasionally rise out of the water to avoid their pursuers, when several of the passengers came to the side on which I was standing to behold a fine-looking vessel which had recently made its appearance. Various were the conjectures as to whither she was bound and to what country she belonged. It was every one's opinion she approached us, and no little pleasure was experienced at the idea of having a vessel so near us, after having been several days without one. The captain seemed alarmed, and kept continually looking at her with his glass, and shortly afterwards the sailors were seen all busy cleaning out the guns, and preparing them for action. By and by it became whispered on board that the vessel was a pirate, and the busy manner in which the seamen were employed at their guns tended to confirm the conjecture. The captain caused all to come on deck. His motives were immediately made out; meanwhile the vessel, which was a good sailer, kept growing nearer, and every thing betokened hostility. We were all in agitation; even the captain and the sailors turned pale with excitement. Every eye was intent on the vessel, and every muscle betokened alarm. She was now within the range of our guns, which were ready for action. At length she hoisted a colour, and immediately a large spreading flag was unfurled on our ship. A breathless silence succeeded; that moment was indescribable. The flags then flying were symbols of peace. Three cheers, spontaneously given, immediately succeeded. A thrill of transport moved the ship, and not a few wept for joy. Our captain, with a trumpet, asked their intentions; he was answered in English from the other ship that they were sailing to the West Indies, and having encountered a storm, they had injured their time-keeper, and could not ascertain their longitude. We gave them all the information they required, and parted with cheerings which were responded to by the other ship, which we soon afterwards lost sight of.[1]

The following day a sailor on the mast announced the appearance of land, a declaration which was eagerly received; during the

[1]The author's recital serves vividly to remind the present-day reader of the fact that barely one hundred years ago the perils of piracy were braved by all who went down to the sea in ships. At least one famous pirate of the gulf region valiantly aided General Andrew Jackson in the defense of New Orleans against British attack in 1814, and for a decade thereafter piracy continued to flourish in the waters adjoining our eastern and southern seaboard.

remainder of the day the passengers were constantly on the look-out, and before night we had the unspeakable pleasure of knowing for ourselves that land was visible. The next day we passed several small islands clad in all the beauty of summer; we were sufficiently near some of them to discover negroes at work besides their little huts, cocoa-nut trees and many other kinds, the names of which I cannot give, being not very near them, and but imperfectly conversant with the productions of tropical regions. The weather was here excessively hot: but a large sail-cloth being put up to shade us from the sun, we almost invariably remained on deck, feasting our eyes with the luxuriant and beautiful appearance of the numerous little islands we were continually passing. I am not aware that the West Indian islands surpass others in beauty, but on account of the length of time we had been without seeing land, we were incessant in our encomiums upon them. Never, thought I, had I seen anything so lovely; I could have wished this the situation of our future abode, this the America so long in anticipation. The two following days no land was visible, a circumstance attended with considerable uneasiness, as we had begun to consider our voyage at an end. On the morning of the third,

however, land was again visible, and this
was America. A sort of melancholy came
creeping over me as I gazed upon it; porten-
tous, perhaps, of the many hardships I was
destined there to endure. We were now in
the mouth of the Mississippi; that night a
large lantern was suspended on the mast, as
a signal for the pilot to come on board and
take charge of the ship. Early the next
morning, while it was yet dark, my husband,
who had been on deck most of the night,
came to invite me thither. I followed him
shortly afterwards, and beheld a fine large
city lighted in a most splendid manner: its
appearance was really brilliant, and gave me
more exalted ideas of the country to which
we were hastening. That morning, by break
of day, a small boat came cutting the water
almost with the speed of the wind; it was
rowed along by four black sailors on each
side; a dignified person was seated in the
midst of them; it was the pilot; he came
alongside the ship, and was taken on board
with his boat and men. After respectful
compliments had passed between him and
the captain, he undertook the management
of the ship, his own sailors obeying his commands, while ours were relieved from duty
to enjoy themselves in chaunting their native melodies, which they did most heartily,

almost to the annoyance of the pilot and his men. This was Sunday morning, the first in November; we had been on board two months and a few days—a period on which I never look back without emotion, as it reminds me of the anxieties I then endured, and of the consequences which that voyage involved.

Chapter 3

AS I intimated in the preceding chapter, we reached New Orleans on Sunday morning; but when I came to survey the town more leisurely, I could scarcely believe it was the Lord's day. I remembered that frequently on our passage I had heard it remarked that the time varied with the time in England a few hours, and for a moment I supposed that the Sabbath varied also. The reader will perceive the cause of my surprise, when he is told that the shops were every where open, stalls set out in all directions, and the streets thronged with lookers-on more in the manner of a fair than a Christian Sabbath. This I was told was the general method of spending that day in New Orleans. With regard to the inhabitants, their appearance was exceedingly peculiar, their complexions varying almost as much as their features; from the deep black of the flat-nosed negro to the sickly pale hue of the American shopman. This city is a regular rendezvous for merchants and tradesmen of every kind, from all quarters of the globe. Slavery is here tolerated in its grossest forms. I observed several groups of

33

slaves linked together in chains, and driven about the streets like oxen under the yoke. The river, which is of immense width, affords a sight not less unique than the city. No one, except eye-witnesses, can form an adequate idea of the number and variety of vessels there collected, and lining the river for miles in length. New Orleans being the provision market for the West Indies and some of the Southern States, its port is frequented not merely by foreign traders, but by thousands of small craft, often of the rudest construction, on which the settlers in the interior bring down the various produce of their climate and industry.[1] The town itself, from its low marshy situation, is very unhealthy; the yellow fever is an everlasting scourge to its inhabitants, annually carrying off great numbers. As a trading port, New Orleans is the most famous and the best situated of any in America; but whoever values a comfortable

---

[1] The flatboat commerce by which the surplus produce of the upper Mississippi Valley was brought to New Orleans flourished for a generation or more, until the era of railroad construction which immediately preceded the Civil War. An Illinois youth of recent adoption who made the long journey to New Orleans the year preceding Mrs. Burlend's arrival in America bore the name of Abraham Lincoln. The journey he made was typical of thousands of similar ones performed in the period here alluded to.

climate or a healthy situation, will not, I am sure, choose to reside there.

But to resume my narrative: having arrived at the port, it was our intention to proceed immediately up the river to St. Louis; but as no steam vessel left till the next day, we remained on board in front of the town. The custom-house officers had not yet been on board to examine the ship, but as we had nothing for which duty would be required, our captain gave my husband a document to present to the inspectors, by which we were allowed to pass early the next morning. Before entering the steam vessel, we got the remainder of our money, all in English sovereigns, exchanged into American dollars. We found that our expenses, since leaving home, amounted to about twenty-three pounds. On leaving the ship I felt a renewal of my home-sickness, to use a quaint expression; it seemed to be the only remaining link between me and England. I was now going to be an alien among strangers. Hitherto I had been accompanied by persons, who when my pain on leaving home manifested itself, could sympathize with me. I should have preferred the meanest passenger on the ship to any I saw on the packet. As, however, we were all in haste to be on our way, I had little time to spend on those tender associations.

A True Picture of Emigration

I certainly left the ship with an aching heart; the captain and cabin passengers had been very kind to us during the voyage, and on going away my children were severally presented with small tokens of approbation, of which they were not a little proud.

I must now leave the ship to pursue my route up the stream of the Mississippi to St. Louis, a distance of not less than thirteen hundred miles. The country on each side of the river is of a dead level, but to all appearance exceedingly productive, and cultivated with considerable pains. On account of the heat which prevails in these districts, the productions of tropical regions are here grown in great abundance. The extensive plantations, notwithstanding their flat appearance, are exceedingly beautiful; and if any thing could have made me forget that I was an unsettled exile, the scenery of the country bordering this river must have done it. There was, nevertheless, one drawback: these beautiful plantations are cultivated by slaves, many of whom we saw as we passed along. As we had regularly to stop by the way to obtain timber for our fires, that being the fuel invariably used by the steamers on this river, we had frequent opportunities of stepping ashore. On one occasion a passenger seeing a negro smoking his pipe by his little cabin, which was just at hand, took the liberty of going up to him for the purpose of begging a little fruit, which hung in plenty on the trees around. The negro, without hesitation, granted his request; and our hero immediately mounted a tree, which he partially stripped of its juicy burden. This little incident might have passed unnoticed, had not the intruder on descending from the tree made use of a kind of box, which was underneath, to break his fall; its structure was too slender for so unusual a load, and in consequence he burst in the top to the terror of the negro, who immediately darted across the orchard, leaving our companion to make the best of his misfortune. The latter was soon convinced that he had committed a blunder, as the box was a bee-hive, and its occupants, aware they had been insulted, would accept no apology, but drawing their sabres attacked their foe with tremendous fury. Poor Yankee was no Leonidas; but with all the speed his heels could muster betook himself to the packet, where he was greeted with roars of laughter by his less enterprising associates.

As we proceeded up the river the country assumed a more rude and uncultivated appearance: the date and plantain tree of the lower regions were exchanged for majestic forest trees and untrodden wilds. Further down it was delightfully pleasant; here magnificently grand eternal forests, in appearance as interminable as the universe, with here and there a patch of ground rudely cultivated by the hand of a lonely settler, constitute the scenery for thousands of miles contiguous to this matchless stream. As to the river itself, I shall not attempt a description of it; what has already been said proves its magnitude to be immensely great; even some of its branches, as the Ohio and the Missouri, are to be classed among the largest rivers in the world. The former[1] is noted for being very muddy, and hurrying in its ungovernable career vast quantities of floating timber, which, decayed by age or other causes, fall into it so as often to render it dangerous for the steamers to pass along. Of these the Mississippi contains acres, that coming from above, have in the lapse of years gradually settled together in places where the current is least active.

Proceeding with my narrative, I must confess I liked the packet much better than I expected. We had engaged to find our own provisions, but on account of their cheapness, or partly because I acted the part of

[1]The river here alluded to is obviously the Missouri, rather than the Ohio.

matron to such as needed my assistance, we were frequently presented with young fowls, coffee, rice, &c., so that our food cost us very little on the river. During this transit we obtained considerable information respecting Illinois, which tended in some degree to lessen our disquietude. We were nevertheless very far from being at ease; our unsettled condition was ever the uppermost in our thoughts, and shed a settled gravity over our conduct. Whilst thus the subjects of painful uncertainty, we were one night much alarmed by the following attempt to rob us: my husband and I were in our berths; I was fast asleep, but he was awake, musing upon our situation, when a black man, one of the crew, knowing we were going to settle in the country, and thinking no doubt we should have money with us, came to the side of our berths and began to search under my pillow, so softly indeed as not to awake me; he was going to examine under my husband's likewise, but as he was awake, he told him he could get him anything he wanted; such unexpected kindness was immediately understood, and the villain disappeared in a moment. Although this attempt proved a complete failure, we were induced to give up our money to the captain the following day, which he kept till we arrived at St. Louis.

A True Picture of Emigration

As my husband kept the money under his pillow, I have never looked back on this circumstance but with feelings of gratitude to Almighty God for his protecting providence, for had he succeeded, we should have been in a most miserable situation, not even able to reach the end of our journey;—destitute and penniless in a strange land, without friends and without home.

The time occupied in passing from New Orleans to St. Louis was about twelve days. We reached the latter place about noon, and found another steamer ready to convey us forward to the situation at which we purposed to remain. I had little opportunity of surveying the town, and therefore can say little respecting it; but was somewhat surprised to find that this noted city should be built principally of wood; its situation is not the most eligible as it regards health, being near the confluence of the Missouri and the Illinois. It is however on that very account likely to become a large and wealthy city, and is indeed by some described as such already.[1] On entering the second steamer I found I had made a poor exchange; the

[1] Although St. Louis dates from 1764, the increase in population was extremely slow for several decades. Upon incorporation as a city in 1823, there were only a few hundred inhabitants. By 1830, the year prior to

40

weather was beginning to feel uncommonly chill, and our accommodation was here very inferior, so that we felt exceedingly anxious to be at our journey's end.

The place at which we intended to leave the river was not more than one hundred and twenty miles from St. Louis; we therefore comforted ourselves with the idea that we should soon be there. We were finally to disembark at Phillip's Ferry, according to the directions sent by the aforementioned Mr. B. to his brother. We should then be within two miles of his residence. Mr. B., therefore, and Phillip's Ferry, occupied our thoughts almost to the exclusion of every other subject. We had already travelled nearly seven thousand miles. Our food had been principally dried provisions. For many long weeks we had been oppressed with anxious suspense; there is therefore no cause for wonder, that, jaded and worn out as we were, we felt anxious to be at our destined situation. Our enquiries of the sailors 'how much further we had to go,' almost exhausted their patience. Already we had been on the vessel twenty-four hours, when just at nightfall the

Mrs. Burlend's visit, the number had increased to almost 5,000. One hundred years later (1930) the U. S. census revealed a population of 821,960, amply fulfilling the forecast of the humble English immigrant of 1831.

A True Picture of Emigration

packet stopped: a little boat was lowered into the water, and we were invited to collect our luggage and descend into it, as we were at Phillip's Ferry;[1] we were utterly confounded: there was no appearance of a landing place, no luggage yard, nor even a building of any kind within sight; we, however,

[1]Philips Ferry is still conducted, on or near the original site, at Valley City, where the present Editor utilized it late in the month of August, 1936. The ferry was established by Garret Van Dusen in 1822, who two years later transferred it to Nimrod Philips.

The latter had come from Kentucky to Pike County about 1821; he died here a decade later. By his will, made in 1826, he bequeathed the ferry to his son, Andrew. This document, still on file in the Court House at Pittsfield, we copy in full for the entertainment of the reader:

"Illinois pike County in the name of God Amen I Nimrod Philips of the State and County aforesaid inten to travel and Not knowing but I may die before I return do make this my last will and testament first I give to Zerrelda Jean my youngest child five head of Cattle a cow cald Cherry and her Caves a horse Cald Jack three beds and furniture and all the kitchen furniture and utensils this I give to my youngest child by Nancy Philips onst Nancy Norris Zerrelda Jean Philips is her name I give to Nancy Philips my wife one loom and its furniture 3 breeding Sows and their pigs six barrows for her meat She is to have her choise of the above named Hoggs She is to live where I now live at the ferry My part of the crop of corn that has been on the place this year to be hers

42

A True Picture of Emigration

attended to our directions, and in a few minutes saw ourselves standing by the brink of the river, bordered by a dark wood, with no one near to notice us or tell us where we might procure accommodation or find harbour. This happened, as before intimated, as the evening shades were rapidly settling on the earth, and the stars through the clear blue atmosphere were beginning to twinkle. It was in the middle of November, and already very frosty. My husband and I looked at each other till we burst into tears, and our children observing our disquietude began to cry bitterly. Is this America, thought I, is this the reception I meet with after my long, painfully anxious and bereaving voyage? In vain did we look around us, hoping to see a light in some distant cabin. It was not, however, the time to weep: my husband determined to leave us with our luggage in search of a habitation, and

She is to live on the place until Zerrelda is of age and have the benefit of the improved land Zerrelda is to have six dolers for 3 years Scholling 18 dollers

I give to Elizabeth Elledge my oldest daughter one doller the rest of my estate and property is to be equaly divided between my 3 children Andrew Philips, Selah Philips, Asa Philips except Andrew is to have the ferry this is my last will and testament wished us to remain where we then stood till he returned. Such a step I saw to be necessary, but how trying! Should he lose himself in the wood, thought I, what will become of me and my helpless offspring? He departed: I was left with five young children, the youngest at my breast. When I survey this portion of my history, it looks more like fiction than reality; yet it is the precise situation in which I was then placed.

After my husband was gone I caused my four eldest children to sit together on one of our beds, covered them from the cold as well as I could, and endeavoured to pacify them. I then knelt down on the bare ground, and committed myself and little ones to the Father of mercies, beseeching him 'to be a lantern to my feet, a light unto my path, and to establish my goings.' I rose from my knees considerably comforted, and endeavoured to wait with patience the return of my husband. Above me was the chill blue canopy of heaven, a wide river before me, and a dark wood behind. The first sound we heard was that of two dogs that came barking towards us, so as greatly to increase our alarm; the dogs came up to us, but did us no harm, and very soon after I beheld my dear husband, accompanied by a stranger, who conducted us to his habitation, whither our luggage was shortly afterwards removed in a waggon.

My husband had followed a sort of cattle track, which led him to the house, which had been concealed by trees and underwood growing around it. And now, for the first time in my life, did I fairly see the interior of a log-house, which, however rude I might think it, I felt, as the reader will readily believe, most happy to enter. It was much more comfortable to sleep on a bed laid on the floor before a fire of glowing embers, than it would have been on the cold ground, which a short time before I feared would be my lodging. The following morning, after a comfortable night's repose, we felt our health and spirits improved. My husband began to examine the soils and produce of the country, and I to collect what information I could respecting American housewifery, manners, religion, &c. Our hostess was a little woman, exceedingly fond of smoking, as the Americans generally are, particularly the females. Before leaving England I had heard a great deal said in behalf of American hospitality, but these encomiums certainly require to be qualified: they are exceedingly hospitable to gentlemen who may be making a tour, likewise amongst themselves as neighbours;

but when they know a person really must
trouble them, they appear to be aware they
are conferring a favour, and expect an equiv-
alent. The little lady I have been describing
knew little of generosity; we understood very
soon that we should be expected to pay for
our harbour, although we used our own provisions. I am forgetting that on one occasion she generously told me I might give my
children the broth in which she had boiled
some cabbage, if I thought they would drink
it; I told her they had not been accustomed
to such fare. We remained here three days,
during which I became tolerably conversant
in the theory of American housekeeping,
and as Mrs. Phillips[1] (that was the name
of our hostess) was very loquacious, she in-
itiated me into the peculiarities of Illinois
politeness. No person, however slender his
pretensions to knighthood, or how long so-
ever the time since his small-clothes were
new, is addressed without the courteous

[1] The will of Nimrod Philips seems to indicate that the
Mrs. Philips whom Mrs. Burlend knew was a second
wife of Nimrod, whose maiden name was Nancy Norris. Of her we have learned nothing apart from the
vivacious picture limned by our author. An earlier wife
of Philips who was a member of the Elledge family in-
termarried with the Boones, and on coming to Illinois
settled in Scott County on the east side of the Illinois
River from Pike.

epithet of 'Sir;' and this practice is observed by the members of the same family
in their intercourse with each other; of
course the females are in like manner honoured with 'Madam,' *Ubi tu Caius, ego
Caia.* It is not etiquette in Illinois to sit
at the table after you have done eating; to
remain after you have finished your meal
implies that you have not had sufficient.
This custom I subsequently found a very
convenient one.

But I am forgetting the house. It was a
fair specimen of a log-house, and therefore a
description of it will give the reader a pretty
correct idea of the American peasantry.
There were two rooms, both on the ground
floor, separated from each other with boards
so badly joined, that crevices were in many
places observable. The rooms were nearly
square, and might contain from thirty to
forty square yards each; beneath one of the
rooms was a cellar, the floor and sides of
which were mud and clay, as left when first
dug out; the walls of the house consisted of
layers of strong blocks of timber, roughly
squared and notched into each other at the
corners; the joints filled up with clay. The
house had two doors, one of which is always
closed in winter, and open in summer to
cause a draught. The fire was on the floor at

the end of the building, where a very gro-
tesque chimney had been constructed of
stones gathered out of the land, and walled
together with clay and mud instead of ce-
ment. It was necessarily a great width, to
prevent the fire from communicating with
the building. The house was covered with
oak shingles; that is to say, thin riven
boards nailed upon each other, so as just to
over-reach. The floors of the house were
covered with the same material, except a
large piece near the fire, which was paved
with small stones, also gathered from the
land. There was no window to the house I
am describing, although many log-houses
may now be found having glass windows.
This inconvenience I pointed out to my hostess, who replied, 'upon the whole it was as
well without, for in winter the house was
warmer and in summer they had always the
door open, which was better than any window.' It is in reality true, that the want of
light is felt very little in a log-house; in
winter they are obliged to keep fine blazing
fires, which, in addition to the light obtained from their low wide chimneys, enable
the inmates to perform any business that is
requisite.

It is however by no means to be understood that an American log house equals in

comfort and convenience a snug English cottage. It is quite common to see, at least, one bed in the same room as that in which the fire is kept; a practice which invariably gives both the bed and house a filthy appearance. There was no chamber, only a sort of loft, constructed rather with a view to make the house warmer, than to afford additional room. Adjoining one side were a few boards nailed together in the form of a table, and supported principally by the timber in the wall. This was dignified with the name 'sideboard.' In the centre of the room, stood another small table, covered with a piece of coarse brown calico; this was the dining table. The chairs, four in number, were the most respectable furniture in the house, having bark of ichory platted for bottoms. Besides these there were two stools and a bench for common use,—a candlestick made from an ear of Indian corn, two or three trenchers and a few tin drinking vessels. One corner of the house was occupied with agricultural implements, consisting of large hoes, axes, &c., for stubbing, called in America grubbing, flails and wooden forks, all exhibiting specimens of workmanship rather homely. Various herbs were suspended from the roof with a view of being medicinally serviceable, also two guns, one of them a rifle. There were

49

also several hams and sides of bacon, smoked almost till they were black; two or three pieces of beef, &c. Under one of the beds were three or four large pots filled with honey, of which Mrs. P. was not a little lavish, as she used it to every meal along with coffee. The furniture in the other room consisted of two beds and a hand-loom, with which the family wove the greater part of their own clothes. In the cellar I observed two or three large hewn tubs, full of lard, and a lump of tobacco, the produce of their own land, in appearance sufficient to serve an ordinary smoker his life.

During our sojourn at Mr. Phillips', my husband found Mr. B., and on the third day after our arrival, brought that gentleman's team, two stiff oxen yoked to a clumsy sledge; on which we placed our beds, boxes, &c. and bid good by to Mrs. P., who, as we paid her for our harbour, contrived to shed a tear or two at the thoughts of parting. After arriving at Mr. B.'s house, I certainly felt I had been a little cajoled. My husband had seen him the day before, but had made no mention of his condition. He was in the fields when we arrived; but as the door was unlocked, or rather lockless, we took the liberty of introducing ourselves and luggage. Mr. B. was at once a bachelor and solitaire.

A True Picture of Emigration

He had left England precipitately, and what is more unusual, a great part of his money, which at this time he was daily expecting by a remittance. The property he had taken with him was all expended in land and cattle, so that a little money was a desideratum. Shortly after our arrival, Mr. B. made his appearance, which, as I before intimated, was rather mysterious. In his letters sent to England, he had spoken of his situation as 'a land flowing with milk and honey'; but I assure you patient reader, his appearance would have led any one to suppose that he gathered his honey rather from thorns than flowers. He was verily as ragged as a sheep: too much so for decency to describe. And his house was more like the cell of a hermit who aims at super-excellence by enduring privations than the cottage of an industrious peasant. The bed on which he slept was only like a bolster which he had used on shipboard, and laid upon a kind of shelf of his own constructing. Then again the walls of his house were of hewn timber as others, but the joinings or interstices were left quite open. The first night I passed in this miserable abode I was almost perished. My husband was obliged to heat a flat iron, and after wrapping it in flannel, apply it to my feet, so little were we protected from the inclemency of the weather. Finding our comforts here so few, we determined to have a home of our own as soon as possible. Mr. B. was too busy in his farm to render my husband much assistance in selecting a piece of ground. Besides the condition of his *haut-de-chausse*[1] rendered it almost imperative upon him to keep near home, especially as he was a bachelor.

Before I proceed any further with my narrative, perhaps it will be of advantage to the reader to explain the method of purchasing land in the United States. The land in the various states has all been surveyed by direction of the government, and divided into portions of eighty acres each. For the sale of the land thus surveyed and laid down on large plans, a land-office is established in various central situations, where all the allotments of a certain district are sold, and the purchasers' names registered. Any person, therefore, who wishes to purchase one or more of these subsections, can see the plan, and select any that are unsold. They will even sell as small a quantity as forty acres; but as they do this merely to accommodate new settlers, no person already possessing eighty acres, can purchase a smaller quantity than that at a time. In some of the

[1] Meaning, his trousers.

older states the government lands are all
sold off. It must there be bought of private
owners; but in Illinois and other new states
there is plenty unsold. The government
price everywhere is one hundred dollars for
eighty acres. As there are myriads of acres
yet in its native luxuriant wildness, any person may with impunity cultivate as much as
he chooses without paying anything; and,
as a further inducement, when a person begins thus to cultivate, no other person can
legally purchase that land, till four years
have expired from the time of his beginning
to cultivate. By obtaining what is termed a
pre-emption the improvement arising from
his own industry is as secure to him for
four years as if he was the actual owner.
Should, however, he fail to pay for the land
before the term expires, an indifferent person may then purchase it; but this seldom
happens. Every person purchasing land at
the office, must declare upon oath, if required, that no other party has an improvement on it. And, if it be proved to be otherwise, such purchase is in every case invalid;
and the fraudulent party liable to a heavy
fine.

An improved eighty acres was the first
land we purchased: we obtained it in the
following manner:—A person named Mr.

A True Picture of Emigration

Oakes[1] having heard that a family about to settle was sojourning at Mr. B.'s came to invite my husband to buy some venison, which he had killed with his rifle just before. My husband went with him, and in conversation found he was disposed to sell his improvement right; for the four years were not expired, and he had not entered it at the land office. For this right he wanted sixty dollars. My husband told him he would call upon him the next day, and returned to Mr. B.'s after buying a quantity of nice venison at a halfpenny per pound. The following day, my husband and I visited at Mr. Oakes's, who took us round the estate,

[1]There were, commonly, three waves of migration in the settlement of any given portion of the frontier. First of all came the traders, hunters, and trappers, with no particular intention of improving the country. Second came the "squatters," who occupied (without troubling to buy legal title) a tract of land and made some slight improvements on it, frequently building a cabin and reducing one or more acres to cultivation, but relying largely upon hunting and on the natural products of the forest for their support. In the wake of the squatter came the permanent settler, who acquired legal title to the soil and developed a home with the intention of passing it on to his children. Oakes, the individual here noted, was evidently a squatter, who has left no record of his sojourn in the community. Of him and his kind, Mr. Jess M. Thompson, local historian, observes, "All seem to have vanished from the community at an early day."

shewed us the boundaries, which were marked out by large stones set at each corner, termed the corner stones.

On the land there were about four hundred sugar maples which Mr. Oakes had tapped the preceding year. These trees grow plentifully in the United States, and promise with proper culture to supersede the use of West Indian sugar in America. They like a low situation and a deep soil, and grow to a larger size than any trees in this country. They are said to thrive the better the oftener they are pierced. The method of obtaining sugar from them is very simple. A small cabin, or, as it is there termed, camp, is built in the midst of the trees; two or three large coppers, holding from five to ten gallons each, are set within it, to boil the liquor, which being drained from the trees into hewn wooden troughs, is carried into the camp. The incisions are made with an auger in the beginning of March, when the sap is beginning to rise. Into each of these holes a tube is inserted, about an inch in diameter, so as just to fill the hole, through this the liquor flows as through a spout. The tree from which these tubes are made, is admirably adapted for the purpose, growing somewhat like the elder, only its branches are straighter and contain more pith. It is usually called in Illinois the shoemaker's tree,[1] its botanical name I do not know. The most suitable weather for the discharge of this liquor is when the days are fine and the nights frosty. After the liquor is thus collected, it is boiled down to the consistency of thin treacle. It is then strained through a coarse woollen cloth, and afterwards boiled again at a slower fire till it becomes hard and firm like raw sugar. It is at present much used in the United States, and always sells at a higher rate than that from the West Indies. On the land now under considera-tion, Mr. Oakes had broken up about twelve acres, three of which were sown with wheat, and the remaining nine ready to be sown with Indian corn, oats, &c. the following spring. As we liked the situation and land very much and were wishful to be settled, the agreement was completed that evening, and the money paid and possession obtained the following day. The reader is aware that the sixty dollars given to Mr. Oakes, were only for his house, improvement right, sugar-making utensils, &c. One hundred more we paid at the land office, at Quincy, and we ob-tained the usual certificate or title deeds; and thus by the first of December, having spent

[1]Apparently the co-author of Mrs. Burlend's narra-tive nodded here. The tree in question is the sumac.

about thirty pounds in travelling, thirty-five
more in land, &c. we were the rightful owners
of a farm of eighty acres, with a log house in
the centre of it.[1] What more could we require? The reader will perceive in the next
chapter.

[1]The farm which the immigrants thus obtained for
their home is legally known as the northeast ¼ of the
northeast ¼ of Section 6, Twp. 5 S, R. 2 W. of the
Fourth P. M. It lies about two miles east of Bethel
Cemetery, and about three miles north of the village of
Detroit, in northwestern Detroit Township. Three
miles to the northeast lies Valley City, formerly Philips
Ferry. The approach of the Burlends to the farm site
was, of course, by way of Philips Ferry. The original
cabin site was on the face of a sloping hillside, a few rods
from a spring which still gives forth a stream of clear,
cool water.

Chapter 4

DURING the time we were at lodgings we had felt ourselves dependent, and looked forward with anxious expectation to the time when we might again taste the sweets and independence of home, and those enjoyments which are only to be expected at one's own fireside. That period had now arrived. We had indeed a house such as I have already described, but we had no furniture except two large boxes, two beds, and a few pots and cooking utensils; besides, our provisions were just finished. Till this time we had been using principally the remains of biscuits, &c., purchased at New Orleans. The first wants of nature must be first attended to: whether we had a chair to sit on or not, something to eat we must have. Our nearest neighbour lived about half-a-mile from us, and we were at least two miles and a-half from any place at which flour was sold; thither, however, my husband went, and as our money was growing scarce, he bought a bushel of ground Indian corn, which was only one-third the price of wheaten flour; it was there sold for thirty cents a bushel. Its taste is not pleasant to persons unaccustomed to it; but as it is wholesome food, it is much used for making bread. We had now some meal, but no yeast, nor an oven; we were therefore obliged to make sad paste, and bake it in our frying pan on some hot ashes. We procured a little milk of our nearest neighbour, Mr. Paddock, which, on account of the severe frosts that prevail in Illinois, we generally received in lumps of ice.

Thus we lived the first few weeks at our new estate. Hasty pudding, sad bread, and a little venison which we had left, were our ordinary food. The greater part of my husband's time was spent in cutting and preparing wood for our fires. About this time we made further purchases of a cow and calf, for which we paid fourteen dollars, a young mare, which cost us twenty dollars, two pigs, and a shallow flat-bottomed iron pan, with a cover to it, to bake in. This is the common, and indeed almost the only kind of oven used in Illinois. It is vulgarly called a skellit. To make it hot it is immersed in glowing embers, the lid is then removed till the dough is put in; it is then replaced and ashes again thrown over it, till the cake is baked. Hence it will be perceived that a quantity of bread beforehand is unknown in Illinois: their custom is to bake a

cake to each meal, which is generally very
good; eggs and milk being so plentiful, are
regularly used in their bread, along with a
little celeratus to lighten it, whereby it becomes very rich and nutritive.

The Illinois settlers live somewhat differ-
ently from the English peasantry; the former
have only three meals a-day, and not much
variety in them: bread, butter, coffee, and
bacon, are always brought to the table, but
fresh meat is a rarity, and is never obtained
as in England by going to a butcher for it.
In Illinois the farmers all kill their own cattle, and salt what is not used immediately;
sometimes, however, they distribute portions among their neighbours, with the view
of receiving as much again when they kill
theirs. It is by no means uncommon for an
old settler to have a couple of fowls, ducks,
a goose, or a turkey to dinner; and, generally
speaking, everybody has plenty of plain good
food. [The object contemplated in this work
requires that I should occasionally leave my
own history, to render more complete the
information I have to impart; I hope, therefore, the reader will not think me incoherent.
To proceed:] we bought the live stock above
described of Mr. Oakes, and as it was winter,
we wanted something with which to feed
them. Indian corn is nearly the only winter

food used in Illinois; and as the culture and management of it occupy a great portion of the farmer's time and industry, it may be not out of place to explain the method of cultivating it: the land intended for Indian corn should be ploughed and harrowed once or twice to make the earth loose and mellow, that the roots may strike with greater freedom; furrows are then made at the distance of about a yard from each other: these are afterwards crossed by other furrows made at right angles to the first, and about the same distance apart; by this means the field appears divided into numberless little square portions, each somewhat less than a square yard as if hollowed at the centre; into each of these crossings four seeds are thrown, and slightly covered with a hoe; this is done in the beginning of March, and after the young blades make their appearance the plough is occasionally drawn along between the rows, for the purpose of checking weeds and keeping the mould as light as possible; as these groups of plants are so far apart, kidney beans, melons, and pumpkins are frequently sown among them, for which the strong stems of the corn are excellent supports.

Indian corn usually ripens about the beginning of October, and is of an immense produce. There are commonly four or five ears to each stem, each ear having from five hundred to a thousand grains in it.[1] As the ears ripen they gradually assume a pendent form, and are in that position severally over-hung with the leaves of the plant, which form a sort of sheath, securely protecting them from rain; in this manner, when prop-erly ripened, it will remain in perfect safety all winter uncut; and it is by no means un-common to sow the land with wheat before the corn crop is all removed. It is not always allowed to ripen; part of the crop is often cut, when the corn is about half-fed, which being dried in the sun, the stem and leaves make excellent hay; in this state it is both hay and corn, and is in fact the only hay the farmer preserves for winter, of which he makes small stacks of a peculiar construc-tion, so as not to require thatching. Noth-ing can be more beautiful than a field of Indian corn in full blossom, and perhaps

[1] It seems probable that Edward Burlend, who never saw America, misunderstood what his mother actually told him concerning the corn crop. A yield of four or five ears of corn to a single stalk is so uncommon that the Editor, who grew up on an Iowa farm cannot re-member ever having seen a single example. The Illinois River bottom land is very rich and still produces splen-did crops of corn, but the statement that a yield of four or five ears to the stalk was common, even a century ago, is evidently erroneous.

nothing in nature displays the munificence of Providence more strikingly than this matchless plant. In order to supply our cattle with winter meat, we applied to Mr. Paddock, our nearest neighbour, who sold us part of a field unreaped; some of it we cut down and took home, the rest we allowed to stand and turned our cattle to it. The reader may think it strange that we should turn cattle into the fields in the depth of winter, especially as the winters are there more severe than in England; it is however the regular custom: the cattle are inured to it, as they are never kept up any part of the year, either day or night. The two pigs we had bought we were obliged to kill shortly after we purchased them, as we wanted them for our own use, and we wished to spare the small stock of Indian corn we had on hand. The reader must also know our money was nearly done: I believe we had not more than four or five dollars remaining; part of it we were obliged to spend in sulphur, to cure what is called the Illinois mange, from which we were all suffering.

This complaint invariably attacks new settlers, shortly after their arrival, and is a complete scourge until it is removed. The body breaks out all over in little spots, attended with intolerable itching. It is generally attributed to the change of water, but as theirs possesses no peculiarity of taste, I cannot understand how that can be the cause. We were soon cured after using the sulphur, and never felt anything more of it.[1]

It has already been said that when we entered our house we had no furniture; this inconvenience my husband, although no joiner, had undertaken to remove, by making for himself and me each a stool, and a low bench for our children, or more properly a log of wood, squared and laid across the hearth for a seat. He had also contrived to make a table, which if not as neat as those used in England, was quite as substantial: having met with a section of a strong tree about two feet long, he rolled it into the house, and set it upon its end; had it been a little longer, its

[1] The "Illinois Mange," a well-known pioneer affliction, as the name itself indicates, seems not to trouble present-day denizens of Pike County. Mr. Francis Allen, a grandson of our author and now eighty years of age, who has lived his entire life in the county, informed the Editor that he had never heard of the disease. Jess M. Thompson, however, local historian (and a great-grandson of Mrs. Burlend) is familiar with its early-day prevalence in the county. He relates that local opinion attributed its occurrence to the rotting of plowed-under vegetation. Another theory attributed its ravages to the decayed fish which perished with the drying-up of ponds along the river bottoms. At Atlas, Pike County, the disease assumed the proportions of an epidemic in 1821, when many of the settlers died from it.

upper surface would have been just what we
wanted; we however nailed a few boards
upon it, making them fit as well as we could,
and having covered it with a cloth to conceal
its roughness, it was far from being con-
temptible, at least for persons like us, who
had been some days without any. As to
bedsteads, we were a few weeks before we
got any; of course we had them to make ourselves, and as we were ill furnished with
tools and unaccustomed to such employment, when they were finished they served
rather to shew how little ornament is absolutely necessary, than our skill as expert car-
penters.

Hitherto the light of the fire had served us
instead of a candle, which was very incon-
venient, as I wished to sew a little in the evenings. It is certainly true that days are
never so short as in England, nevertheless
we were very wishful to have some candles.
The inhabitants commonly make their own,
in tin moulds; but as we had neither moulds
nor tallow, we were obliged to put a little
lard into a saucer, and light a piece of rag
previously inserted in it; by this we could see
to sew and read pretty well; but as the rag
frequently got immersed in the melted lard
it was very troublesome, and by constant
use we had three or four saucers broken with

the heat, a circumstance much to be regretted, as pots of all kinds are dear in Illinois. To prevent a recurrence of this misfortune we ultimately made use of our kettle lid, inserting the knob or holder into a piece of board to make it stand.

Our next great inconvenience was want of soap: having however learnt from Mrs. Phillips the method of making it, we were by this time in a state of readiness for supplying ourselves. The reader will remember we had before this time killed two pigs, the entrails of which we had cleaned and preserved, along with the bits of offal, rendering, scraps, &c., and now the finest of our ashes were collected and put into a large wooden trough, and boiling water poured over them, whence we obtained a strong solution of potash, which we poured off and boiled down; fresh ashes were then used as before, and a fresh solution obtained; the whole was next boiled down to about one third of the original quantity, by which means the solution became so caustic, that it would have taken the skin off one's fingers in a moment. In this state the waste meat and entrails were mixed with it, which it very soon assimilated. After it had obtained the consistency of soft soap, it was poured into a vessel appropriated for the purpose, to be ready for use.

A True Picture of Emigration

This is the manner the American peasantry supply themselves with soap. Their practice of burning wood furnishes them with potash, which they saturate with other ingredients as above described. Since we were thus obliged to provide necessaries for ourselves in a manner very different from that to which we had been accustomed in England, it may be asked if there are no shops in that country. Illinois, it must be known, is very thinly populated, and on that account it is not the situation for shopkeepers. There are, however, in various places, what are termed store keepers, who supply the settlers with articles the most needed, such as food, clothing, implements of husbandry, medicine, and spirituous liquors: for which they receive in exchange the produce of their farms, consisting of wheat, Indian corn, sugar, beef, bacon, &c. As these storekeepers exercise a sort of monopoly over a certain district, their profits are great, and they often become wealthy. Besides their store, they often have a saw-mill and a corn-mill, at which they grind the corn they obtain from the farmers, for the purpose of sending it to New Orleans, or some other place where it can be readily sold. Stores therefore are in Illinois, nearly what markets are in England, only there is more barter in the former country. The mills in that neighbourhood are chiefly turned by water.

We were destined to be unfortunate with the young mare we had purchased of Mr. Oakes. Having been accustomed to run in the fields with other horses, she would not settle with our cow and calf. Every day she was lost; no fences could turn her. We were therefore obliged to sell her, or rather exchange for one not near so good; only she was expected to have a foal the following spring. Shortly after we had parted with the young mare, my husband found two strange horses in the field feeding upon our corn, he turned them out and returned home. On going to the field again they were there a second time; he felt assured some one had turned them in, as the fences were all good. The next morning explained the circumstance, for the horses being in the field as before, he was about to drive them out, when a tall man hastened towards him, and bade him desist, telling him that the horses were his and he intended them to be there. My husband remonstrated with him on the injustice of such behaviour, and persevered in his attempts to drive them out; at which the person, whose name was Brevet, went up to him, and struck him a blow on the forehead with his fist, and threatened further violence

if he did not allow them to remain. Seeing
that physical force was the only available
argument, my husband began to prepare for
resistance; but calling to mind the situation
of his family, and not knowing what perfidy
might be resorted to, he wisely concluded to
leave the man and his horses where they
were. I mention this circumstance principally to shew how much we were indebted to
an over-ruling Providence for the preserva- √
tion of my husband's life on this occasion.
We afterwards learnt that Brevet was a pest
to the neighbourhood, and that he had told
one of his acquaintances of this interview,
and declared he would have stabbed my
partner with a large dirk which he always
carried with him, if he had resisted. In a
short time afterwards he left the neighbourhood, dreaded or detested by all who knew
him.

We have already seen that considerable
labour is required to prepare fuel, as a good
fire in America is essential during the winter
season. The frosts are intensely keen, a wide
river is sometimes iced over in a single night,
so as to be unnavigable. Every thing of a
fluid nature, exposed to the weather, is
formed into a solid. For two or three months
the milk freezing as soon as it is taken from
the cows, affords no cream, consequently no

butter. It is nevertheless possible to obtain butter, by keeping the churn near the fire, and churning cream and milk both together; but as this method is exceedingly trouble-some it is seldom practised. The nights in winter are at once inexpressibly cold, and poetically fine. The sky is almost invariably clear, and the stars shine with a brilliancy entirely unknown in the humid atmosphere of England. Cold as it was, often did I, dur-ing the first winter, stand at the door of our cabin, admiring their lustre and listening to the wolves, whose howlings, among the leaf-less woods at this season, are almost unceas-ing. These animals are numerous in Amer-ica; and, unless the sheep be regularly folded, their depredations are extensively injurious, as they lacerate the throats of nearly all the flock; sometimes also they will seize young pigs, but as they fear the old ones, unless they are impelled by hunger, these animals are not in much danger. The timid submis-sive sheep is always their favourite prey.

The reader will perceive we had not much intercourse with the rest of the world. For a while no one seemed to notice us, except Mr. B., our neighbour Mr. Paddock, and one Mr. Burns, who lived about two miles off, (all are *Misters* in America.) But indeed the villainous conduct of Mr. Brevet had made us so suspicious, that we scarcely knew whether to wish for an increased circle of acquaintance, or entire seclusion. One thing was very afflictive, our being deprived of Christian Sabbath ordinances. We always honoured that day, by abstaining from our accustomed labour; we read our Bible, and meditated thereon: but Sabbath after Sabbath passed away without our once being able to assemble with those who 'keep holy day,' or in the great congregation to unite our tribute of praise, with the aspirations of those whose sentiments are 'how amiable are thy tabernacles O Lord of Hosts!' At this time we were five miles from any place where public worship was regularly conducted; subsequently preaching-houses much nearer were opened, the character of which will be noticed in its proper place.

The motives which occasioned this work to be written require that a strict regard to truth be maintained; and, in matters of fact, that nothing be introduced calculated to mislead, either by deterring or alluring; this rule has hitherto been carefully observed. Am I then asked if we thus far were satisfied with the step we had taken, my answer is, we regretted it very much. We had indeed plenty of corn-bread and milk, but neither beer nor tea; coffee was our chief beverage,

which we used very sparingly, for want of
money. All the water we wanted we had to
thaw, and during the nights, on account of
the severe frosts, we were very cold indeed;
although we always kept the fire burning.
Our bed-clothes we had taken with us from
England, and we were unable to procure any
more, as they were dear, and our means
almost exhausted. We had indeed some
good land, but it was nearly all uncultivated,
and we had nothing to sell except our cattle,
which we wanted. The only ground of hope
we had was in our industry and perseverance. My husband worked very hard; the
little time we had to spare, after feeding the
cattle and procuring fuel, was spent in splitting trees to make rails. All the fences here
are made of rails, there are no thorns in the
neighbourhood. The method of fencing is
peculiar: they use no posts; but having prepared their rails, they lay one down on the
ground, where they wish to make a fence;
not precisely in the same direction as the line
of their intended fence, but making a small
angle with it. Another rail is then laid down
with its end overreaching the first, with
which it forms a cross like the letter X, only
instead of the crossing being at the centre,
it is near the end of each rail. A third is then
made to cross the second as before, and so on

to an indefinite length. On each side of these several crossings a stake is driven into the ground to prevent their being removed. Other rails are then placed upon these, crossing each other in a similar manner, till the fence is as high as it is required. Generally they are about nine rails high. From the description here given, the reader will perceive that the fences are not straight as in England, but in a continued zig-zag. The reason for this difference is, timber and land are of comparatively little value in America, while their method requires less labour than ours.

In this manner we spent our first winter; we had plenty of work; our amusements even tended to advantage. Great numbers of quails frequented our home-stead to feed on our small stock of Indian corn; we caught several of them with snares, which were excellent eating. My husband also shot a few rabbits, of which there are vast numbers in America. We likewise saw several deer, but as we had no rifle, we could not kill any. We observed several kinds of birds, which we had not before seen, one in particular, which we took to be a species of turkey, engaged our attention; my husband tried several times to kill one, without effect. One Saturday, however, he was successful, and brought

73

home his game with as much apparent consciousness of triumph, as if he had slain some champion hydra of the forest. The following day we expected Mr. B., who by this time had received his money, to dine with us. We accordingly dressed our bird, and congratulated ourselves with the idea of having our countryman to dine with us on a fine boiled turkey. Sunday morning arrived, and in due time our turkey was in the pot boiling for dinner. Mr. B. came; we told him how happy we were on account of the treat we were going to give him. He was surprised at our story, as those birds are difficult to obtain with a common fowling-piece, and desired to see the feet and head. But the moment he saw them, he exclaimed 'it's a buzzard,' a bird which, we subsequently learnt, gormandizes any kind of filth or carrion, and consequently is not fit to be eaten. We were sorely disappointed; our turkey was hoisted into the yard, and we were obliged to be contented with a little bacon, and a coarse Indian corn pudding, for which our stomachs were not altogether unprepared, although recently in anticipation of more sumptuous fare. The reader may think we were stupid not to know a turkey; the bird in question is very much like one, and indeed on that account is called in Illinois a turkey-buzzard.

A True Picture of Emigration

As spring approached we felt some symptoms of those hopes which had animated us
in England with reference to our success as
emigrants. Man's career in prospective is
always brilliant; and it is providentially ordered that it should be so. Could we have
foreseen our destiny, the prospect would
have thrown us into despair. It would have
robbed us of much present enjoyment, and
unfitted our minds for the difficulties with
which we had to struggle. I am, however,
anticipating my history. The symptoms to
which I referred originated with the idea of
being the cultivators of our own land. How
those prospects were realized, the sequel will
explain. By the beginning of March our
Indian corn was done, and it had served so
long only through the greatest care. There
was however by this time a little fresh grass
in the woods, to which we were very glad to
turn our little stock, consisting as before
stated of a cow and calf, and a mare near
foaling. As this method of summering cattle
in America is peculiar to that country, and
affords to the farmer considerable advantages, I shall endeavour to be explicit in the
account of it, which I am about to give. I
must then premise that all unenclosed lands,
whether purchased of government or other- √
wise, are considered common pasturage; and

as there are in Illinois thousands of acres in
that state, any person can keep as many
cattle during summer as he chooses. They
are turned out at spring, and thus run where
they please. A person unacquainted with
these habits would naturally be afraid of
losing them in such immeasurable regions.
This, however, seldom happens. There are
few animals having a sufficiency of food that
are fond of ranging over strange domains.
Even in this country we observe foxes and
hares to have their favourite haunts, from
which it is difficult to break them. Domesti-
cated animals manifest this principle of attachment still more strongly. Hence no
American farmer, having his cattle on the
range, would fear being able to find them in
a few hours; and indeed a person unacquainted with the haunts of any certain
herd, would most probably go directly towards them. Rivers and smaller streams
have certainly some confining influence, but
independent of that, their habits are to frequent those situations only to which they
are accustomed. In that country cattle have
a great liking for salt, and indeed it seems
essential to their health, particularly in summer. An English farmer would smile to see
a herd of cattle contending with each other
over a few handfuls of dry salt which had

been thrown on the floor for them. This is seen every day in America. The milch cows require more of it than the rest, and unless they are regularly served with it, their milk becomes unpleasant. This induces them to come to their stand to be milked twice-a-day. Oxen and heifers will take no harm if they have a little twice-a-week, or even not so often. Where so many different herds of cattle run at large, there is a greater danger of their intermixing than of their being lost. To prevent this, great care is taken by each grazier at the spring to mark his own. Some cut their ears in various ways. Others burn certain marks on their horns with a hot iron. There is not, however, much confusion. The cattle which have been fed together during winter, most generally associate with each other in summer; all having an unaccountable attachment to the master beast of the herd, apparently considering his presence a source of protection or honour. For this reason the owner usually suspends a bell round this animal's neck, which enables him to find his cattle with greater ease. Hence the phrase, 'bear the bell,' is common even in this country. In this manner the cattle graze during summer, and when the pasturage fails, they cease to range; but besetting their master's cabin with incessant lowings

remind him that winter is approaching, and
that their claims to his bounty deserve attention, and must have it. At this time if
any strange cattle have joined the herd, the
law requires that the farmer cause them to
be valued, and their mark to be taken down
and sent to four of the nearest mills for publicity; if they are not owned within a year
they belong to the herd.

I must now leave our small herd of cattle
running in the woods, to acquaint the reader
with our first summer's performances and
success. The first fruits of our industry were
derived from our sugar orchard, the care of
which devolved principally on me. We were
in want of nearly all kinds of implements of
husbandry, without the means of procuring
them, except by running into debt, a practice which we felt reluctant to adopt. Our
sugar trees therefore at this time afforded us
a seasonable boon. The weather was favourable, and by hard working we made nearly
three hundred weight, besides a barrel of
molasses. We disposed of the greater part
of it to a store-keeper named Mr. Varley, at
the rate of seven or eight cents per pound. It
must not be understood that we got money
for it. Business is seldom transacted after
that manner in Illinois. My meaning is we
were allowed to take anything we wanted

from the store by paying for it with sugar at the above rate. Our first care was to have some Indian corn for seed, and some more meal for our own use, which at that time we wanted. We likewise obtained a little coffee, two or three hoes, and a Yankee axe, which is much larger and broader than the one used in this country, and better adapted for the every-day business of hewing large blocks of timber for fuel and other purposes.

And now, kind reader, if thou hast any intentions of being an emigrant, I cordially wish thee success; but before thou forsakest the endearments of thy present home, consider the situation in which we were placed with a helpless family dependent upon us. Thou hast seen us expend our little money with the utmost frugality; thou art acquainted with our possessions, real and personal. It was now the middle of March, when Indian corn, the most useful produce of that country, must be sown, or the season would be past. We had land and seed, but no plough, nor any team, except an old mare, that we feared would scarcely live while she foaled, and consequently we could not yoke her. What could we do? If we did not sow we could not reap; we should have nothing to feed our cattle with the ensuing winter. *Labor omnia vincit* was our motto. We set

to work with our hoes; I, husband, and son,
the latter under ten years of age, and day
after day, for three successive weeks, did we
toil with unwearied diligence till we had
sown and covered in nearly four acres. We
should probably have sown more, had not
the rains which fall in torrents at this season
prevented us. Whilst referring to the
weather, it will be proper to observe that
during the month of April in Illinois, a great
quantity of rain usually falls, accompanied
almost invariably with thunder storms of a
most awful character. A person who has
lived only in England can have but an im-
perfect conception of these electrical phenomena. They happen most frequently in
the night, which considerably increases their
power of striking terror through the most
intrepid bosom. The weather is at this time
close and sultry, and as the sun declines the
sky becomes gradually overcast; midnight
arrives, a pitchy darkness overhangs the
earth; by and by the wind begins to roar in
the trees, and the hoarse thunder in the distance announces the coming of the storm.
As it approaches the thunder claps wax
louder and louder, while the lightning begins to play across the gloomy firmament,
in a most awful and terrific manner. Every
moment the voice of the thunder acquires

additional compass, never ceasing even for a moment; but before one peal has well broken on the ear, it is drowned by another still more tremendous and loud. The lightning is even more overpowering than the thunder. One moment all is in obscurity, a second the heavens seem rent asunder, the bright blue lightning dancing in all directions with a frightful and deadly velocity; meanwhile the rain descends in torrents, threatening to sweep away the foundation of the dwelling. The length of time these storms continue is generally about an hour. The first I witnessed made an impression on my mind that will never be forgotten; my senses were completely disordered: I became alarmed at the slightest noise, and for a while felt more afraid of a thunder storm than of any calamity which appeared in the power of misfortune to inflict upon me. Probably my late anxieties and bereavement preying on my mind had indisposed my nerves for such phenomena, at once terrific, awful, and sublime. But whatever was the cause, I have great pleasure in stating that I soon got the better of my timidity. Trees have frequently been struck near our house, but hitherto no accident has befallen us. We now consider these storms rather as annoying than dangerous; one reason perhaps is that a dry log house is a bad conductor of the electric fluid.

About this time we were sorely tormented with another scourge, which unlike the one just noticed, possessed exceedingly little of a poetical or sublime character. It certainly operated on the nerves powerfully enough, but that in a manner rather calculated to move the lower than the more elevated passions of our nature. I refer to the musquitoes; swarms of which infest that country during spring and autumn, much to the annoyance of its inhabitants. This troublesome insect is not unlike the gnat, which in this country so often terminates its existence by flying into the candle. Its bite is slightly venomous, causing small blisters somewhat like those occasioned by the sting of a nettle, only the pain attending it is more acute. They are the most numerous in low situations, or among thick woods where the heat is less oppressive. This insect cannot bear great heats, and on that account is never seen during the hottest weather, except in very shady places. It is always most troublesome in the nights; and as it makes a constant humming when it flies, it is a most noisy as well as a most unwelcome guest in a lodging room. I do assure the reader I have lain for hours together with a handkerchief in my hand, fanning them from my face, when a little sleep would have been a more seasonable relaxation. Various methods are practised to drive them off or avoid them. We frequently made a fire at the door, and covered it with green leaves to make as much smoke as possible, and thereby to banish them from the neighbourhood; but the moment the smoke was dissipated they again made their appearance as numerous as flies in England on a summer day. Many persons make what are termed musquito hangings for their beds; these are constructed of laths strung together so closely as not to allow a space for them to pass through. They seldom are seen on the prairies, or indeed in any place remote from thick shady woods; thus some of our neighbours have been quite free from them, while we were tortured incessantly. We however had the advantage of being near fuel, a consideration of great importance in that country, especially as the soil of wood land is always more valuable than that of the prairies, and when cleared is likewise free from musquitoes.

Having referred to the prairies, it may perhaps be necessary to be a little more explicit. Many persons in England have a wrong idea of the uncultivated lands in

America, imagining they are all wood. This is by no means the case. In Illinois there are thousands of acres with not a tree upon it, but covered with a sort of strong wild grass, growing sometimes three or four feet high. These lands are termed prairies, and require only to be broken up with a prairie plough, and they become at once fine arable land. As I before intimated, this kind of land, though the soonest cultivated, is not the most productive being, as the farmers term it, of a stronger quality than the other. The soil of both prairies and woodland is quite black, probably owing to the vegetable matter, which for ages has decayed thereon. At the season of the year now under notice, these prairies present to the eye a most charming appearance. Let the reader imagine himself by the side of a rich meadow, or fine grass plain several miles in diameter, decked with myriads of flowers of a most gorgeous and varied description, and he will have before his mind a pretty correct representation of one of these prairies. Nothing can surpass in richness of colour, or beauty of formation many of the flowers which are found in the most liberal profusion on these extensive and untrodden wilds. The naturalist would here meet with abundance of materials for his genius to arrange,

while the poet, reminded of his elegies, would
perceive how—

"Many a flower is born to blush unseen,
And waste its sweetness on the desert air."

In contrasting the hues of flowers grown in
America with those in England, I must ac-
knowledge that the former country presents
the more splendid; but if they are superior in
colour, they are much inferior in odour. Perhaps the superabundance of light and heat,
which produces such fine colour, is prejudicial to the production of odoriferous plants,
as any thing at all approaching the fragrance
of the honey suckle or sweet briar, I never
witnessed in America. In the woody districts, the trees most commonly met with
are the oak, ichory, walnut and sugar maple,
besides a great deal of underwood and wild
fruit trees of the plum family. As all these
grow in a wild state, it is not to be supposed
that the trees are as numerous as they are in
the plantations of this country. The strong
timber trees grow at various distances from
each other, sometimes being as near to each
other as they can possibly grow, at others
twenty or thirty yards apart. They not only
vary considerably in this respect, but also in
magnitude and age. Not a few are to be
found in the last stage of decay, their patri-
archal dignity gradually submitting to the

all-subduing influence of time. Numbers more are quite hollow, in which bees, owls, and rabbits severally find shelter and propagate their species. Every thing here bears the mark of ancient undisturbed repose. The golden age still appears, and when the woodman with his axe enters these territories for the first time, he cannot resist the impression that he is about to commit a trespass on the virgin loveliness of nature, that he is going to bring into captivity what has been free for centuries.

In resuming the thread of my narrative, I have to state, that as soon as we had sown our Indian corn, and planted a few potatoes, we began to prepare for taking in more land, although we had four or five acres unsown of that which Mr. Oakes had broken up. We hoped, nevertheless, that before another season we should be able to plough and sow in a regular manner. Accordingly my husband worked hard every day with his grubbing hoe and axe, tearing up the roots of underwood and cutting down some of the largest trees. When trees are cut down in America, as little regard is paid to the timber, they do not cut them off level with the ground as in England, but about three feet from it. The remaining part is burnt after it has been exposed to the sun's rays a few months. Many

trees however are allowed to remain standing, after the bark has been cut, to cause
them to die. In this state they remain even
after the land is sown, for, being destitute of
foliage, they do no harm to the crop.

While my husband was thus engaged I
frequently went to him, and, assisted by our
little boy, gathered the most portable pieces
of brushwood, and took them to our cabin to
be ready for fuel; thus, by continued exer-
tions, we had cleared three or four acres by
the end of May, and made a fence half round
the piece we intended to enclose as our next
field, consisting of about eight acres. Before
this time our old mare had foaled, and as we
partly expected, only survived that event a
few weeks. Near our house there is a sort of
rivulet, termed in Illinois a branch, in which
one Sunday evening, after we had walked
ten miles in going to and from the chapel, we
found her laid; we got her out with the help
of a rope, and after a while she appeared
little worse; a week or two afterwards, however, her foal came by itself neighing to our
door; we were immediately assured that
something had befallen its mother, and set
out in search of her, whither the foal, going
before, led us as naturally as if it had been
endowed with reason; she had again fallen
into the branch, and was quite dead. The

foal, notwithstanding its loss, throve very well, and subsequently became a very valuable brood mare.

In the month of June, notwithstanding our economy, we were obliged to purchase some meal on credit. Mr. Varley, the storekeeper, very willingly allowed us to have as much as we wanted, and indeed offered to sell us anything else on the same terms. His miller, however, as soon as he knew we were not giving ready money, only partly filled the bushel, thereby making it dearer to us than before, and we dared not complain to his master for fear he should refuse it altogether. The debt we contracted was very small,—not a dollar—for which we had bread for the family not less than six weeks; the expiration of which brings us to the end of our first wheat harvest, a season conspicuous in my history on account of the severe trials I then experienced.

Chapter 5

TOWARDS the end of June our three acres of wheat began to look ripe, and we consequently had to consider how we should reap it; we had no sickles, nor were any to be had under a dollar each; we therefore, self and husband, resolved to go to our friend Mr. B., who lent us two, for which we were thankful enough, although they were poor ones. As we were returning home, my husband had the misfortune to stumble over a log of wood, and having a sickle in his hand, he pitched upon the edge of it with his knee, and cut it severely. We were then a mile from home, and the wound bled profusely. I bound it up with a handkerchief, and after a little faintness he was able to proceed. The next day, on examining the cut, we found it to be more serious than we had imagined: the symptoms were also bad; instead of being warm and irritable, it was cold and numb. In vain did we apply lotions, it kept growing worse and worse. The following day it began to swell very much, and to be exceedingly painful at a distance from the cut. The pain took away his appetite for food, and symptoms of inflammation and fever became rapidly apparent. My situation requires no comment: I could not but perceive I was likely to lose my dearest earthly friend, and with him all visible means of supporting myself, or maintaining my family. I was almost driven to frenzy. Despair began to lay hold of me with his iron sinews; I longed to exchange situations with my husband; there was no one near to assist or encourage me. My eldest child alone manifested any signs of sympathy: the poor boy went up to his father's bed, and with affectionate and child-like simplicity said, 'don't die, father, don't die.' Meanwhile the swelling increased; my husband had taken nothing but a little coffee for two days. Here was a crisis: I saw a short time would determine whether I was to be reduced to a situation the most wretched imaginable, or see my husband restored to me again. The latter idea seemed to contain all I had in this world to cling to. I could not give it up. I fomented the swelling with increased diligence, till at length he began to perspire, and his leg to possess its wonted sensibility. A change for the better had evidently taken place, and by degrees all the bad symptoms disappeared.

On perceiving this, I felt myself the happiest woman on earth, although my situation was still embarrassing. Our wheat was quite ripe, indeed almost ready to shake, and if not cut soon, would be lost. We had no means of hiring reapers, and my husband could not stir out. I was therefore obliged to begin myself; I took my eldest child into the field to assist me, and left the next in age to attend to their father and take care of the youngest, which was still unweaned. I worked as hard as my strength would allow; the weather was intolerably hot, so that I was almost melted. In little more than a week, however, we had it all cut down. Meanwhile my husband had continued to mend, and was now able to leave his bed and sit in a chair, or rather on a stool placed near the wall for support to his back, and made further comfortable with the help of a pillow or two. The wheat was still unhoused, and exposed to the rays of the burning sun, by which it was in danger of being dried so as to waste on the slightest movement. It was absolutely necessary that it should be gathered together forthwith. Having neither horses nor waggon, we here encountered another difficulty. The work, however, could not be postponed. With a little trouble I got two strong rods, upon which I placed a number of sheaves near one end of them; I then caused my little son to take hold of the lighter end, and in this manner we gathered together the whole of the three acres. My partner had by this time so far recovered as to be able to move about with the help of a strong staff, or crutch, and thus he came to the door to shew me how to place the sheaves in forming the stack. The reader may probably suppose I am endeavouring to magnify my own labours, when I tell him I reaped, carried home, and stacked our whole crop of wheat, consisting, as before stated, of three acres, with no other assistance than that of my little boy under ten years of age.

My statements are nevertheless uncoloured facts, and what renders them still less credible, the work was performed in addition to the attendance necessarily required by my young family and sick husband, and during the hottest part of the year, in a climate notorious for excessive heat. I would not be understood to represent the climate of Illinois as greatly prejudicial to the health of English emigrants. My health had hitherto been much better there than in England, a circumstance which I attribute in part to the beneficial effects of the voyage, but still more to the difference in the state of the atmosphere between America and England. The reader must know that previous to leaving this country I was slightly affected with asthmatic symptoms, which entirely left me for a number of years after my arrival in America. A dry air is always allowed to be favourable to persons troubled with the above disease; and it is no less notorious that the atmosphere of England is comparatively moist and humid, its insular situation being probably a principal cause. Physical causes, however, I pretend not to understand; I merely refer to them because they seem to bear upon the facts I have to narrate, and because I deem it necessary to be precise and perspicuous on a subject of such importance to the emigrant as is the climate of the country to which his capabilities may be invited. The atmosphere of Illinois then is much drier than that of the British islands. This is apparent from the comparatively few rainy days that occur in that country: in summer the droughts are excessive and long, from which the corn crops sometimes suffer severely; and in winter, during the two coldest months, scarcely any rain falls. Spring and autumn are often very rainy; but, even then, the number of fine days is not less than those in England during the same season. When it does rain it falls in torrents, and is generally accompanied with thunder and lightning, as before stated; a circumstance which corroborates the statements above-named relative to the dryness of the air. A continental situation like that of Illinois must necessarily be affected with greater extremes of heat and cold than a country surrounded by water like Britain. The influence of the sun's rays in the latter place is considerably diminished by the process of evaporation, for which such facilities are offered where water abounds; while on the other hand the cold is less intense on account of the abundance of caloric given out by water to the superincumbent air, when the temperature of the latter descends below the freezing point.

The striking difference between the climate of America and England therefore is, that the extremes of heat and cold are considerably greater in that country than in this; hence tobacco and cotton may be cultivated with success, though the climate in Illinois is scarcely hot enough for the latter; every farmer, however, cultivates tobacco for his own use, in the same manner as the peasants in this country grow cabbages and potatoes; it is sown in beds like onions, at the spring of the year, and though of all seeds apparently the slowest to manifest the vegetative principles, when it has begun to put forth its leaves it grows with unaccountable rapidity. At this period of its growth it is

much infested with a species of green cater-
pillar of an enormous size, from whose ravages the plants require to be daily protected,
or they would shortly disappear. When ripe
its appearance is very much like that of the
rhubarb cultivated in our cottage gardens in
England after it has seeded, only the leaves
of the tobacco plant are larger and not so
heavy. In this state they are cut and dried
in the sun a day or two, and afterwards
gathered together to cause them to sweat,
which gives them that peculiar fragrance
common to tobacco.

As a further illustration of the temperature of the climate, it may be remarked that
melons, pumpkins, cucumbers and peaches
ripen early without any assistance from art.
The woods abound with wild plum-trees, for
which the climate is nevertheless too hot, as
they frequently wither on the trees before
they are fully ripe, and are eaten by pigs, or
remain to decay and fertilize the ground.
Grapes, strawberries and raspberries likewise grow wild in great abundance; the settlers gather them near their houses, in order
to make wine of them; but there are thousands of bushels left to decay where they
grew, after birds and insects have devoured
as many of them as they choose. The raspberries are of a different species from those

grown in England; the bushes themselves are quite similar in appearance, and the flavour of the fruit not much different; but when the berries are ripe they are quite black like the fruit of the bramble. Of all the fruits that are met with in the woods, nuts are the most plentiful; hazels and filberts are found in all directions. During the first two years of our residence in that country my children gathered bushels of them, and even recently I have often been surprised that no bad consequences have ensued from the quantities they have eaten. There are two different kinds of walnut, termed the black and the white walnut, and indeed the ichory is considered as belonging to the same genus, but its fruit is different.

Notwithstanding the beauty and luxuriance of the vegetable productions of Illinois, the summary account here given being a mere sketch, the animal kingdom is still more remarkable for numbers and variety. The naturalist must not search for entertainment in the description about to be given: as a common and unscientific observer I saw and admired them, and as such alone I am able to describe them.

America is certainly and emphatically the country for the feathered tribe, whether numbers, variety, or beauty be the subject of special consideration; nor will any one wonder that they are so numerous when he considers the comparative safety with which they rear their young, and the abundance of food that must be found in a country highly productive, whose seeds and fruits are the undisputed property of the first finder. During the breeding season, their noise, I cannot call it music, is, in the woods, one continued gabble; as their species are so numerous, their tones possess every degree of hoarseness, chatter and chirp, that can possibly be' conceived. To represent their performances in writing is a thing absolutely impossible, especially to persons accustomed to identify their vocal powers with something like music. Some idea of their noise may be gathered by imagining an assembly consisting of magpies, jays, and turkeys, together with a few of the minor species as the gold-finch, the spink, and the sparrow, all giving full play to their vocal energies, and each endeavouring to make his own favorite note as significant as possible; there is nothing of that fine flowing sweetness with which the "early lark" and "sooty blackbird" announce the approach of summer in this country. But if their voices like that of the peacock are offensive to the ear; like that majestic bird's their plumage is exceedingly

beautiful. I must not be understood to in-
clude all kinds of birds met with in Illinois,
in the description now given; one kind is
completely black like the rook, and this sort
is a downright pest to the ripe and ripening
crops; assembling in flocks almost like a
cloud, they require all the farmer's vigilance
to prevent their flying away with the fruits
of his industry. Of the parrot, the owl, and
the jay families there are great numbers,
but the humming bird is the most interesting little bird of any I notice, of which there
are hundreds buzzing about during the summer season. As it would be out of keeping
with the character of this work to describe
the peculiar habits of the various classes of
birds seen in America, I deem it unnecessary
to give the names by which they are known
among the unlettered inhabitants of Illinois, especially as those names are mostly
provincial terms; notwithstanding they are
so numerous there are very few that I could
recognize as species common in my own
country. In vain did I listen for the cuckoo
at the spring of the year, and happy should
I have been to see the tame confiding red-
breast hopping about our door, but it never
appeared.

Proceed we next to notice another class of
animals, which, though not as numerous as

the one just described, are now by no means
rare during warm weather in Illinois: snakes
are the creatures now referred to, of which
there are not only a great variety, but vast
numbers of each species, many of which are
exceedingly venomous. One kind called the
black snake, *alias* the racer, is noticed for
pursuing people who may chance to come
near them during the breeding season; it is
large and completely black, its bite is not
venomous, nor does it attempt to pursue in-
truders, unless they shrink from its intimi-
dating appearance, and even then it generally
returns to its post as soon as it fancies it has
driven them off; sometimes however, it will
wrap round a person's legs, and if the individual in that situation attempts to fly, he
is almost sure to fall; he may however, soon
release himself with a small stick or a knife;
as it is the only snake in America that will
approach man without being previously irri-
tated, it is fortunate that its bite is not venomous: one kind about the size of a small eel
is able to raise itself nearly in a perpendicu-
lar direction; when struck it immediately
appears to be broken or disjointed into three
or four pieces not unlike the herb or weed
termed foxtail, when its joints are disunited;
a third called the copperhead has a most
angry appearance, and its bite is venomous,

but it usually endeavours to get away on the approach of man. The species are too numerous for me to attempt to enumerate them here; it seldom happens that any one is injured by them, but as they are known to lurk in concealed situations, hollow trees, and some even among the branches, they cause people to be constantly on their guard when they have to enter situations favorable for them to lie in.

The rattlesnake, however, is not to be despised, for although it is not so numerous as some of the other kinds, it is more dreaded than them all; this formidable foe never attacks man except in self-defence, and then its bite, if no antidote be taken, is speedily fatal. The usual medicine given to a person thus bitten, is a strong infusion of a herb called the rattlesnake's master. The rattle from which the reptile has its name, is situated at the end of its tail, and composed of thin hollow bones articulated so as to make a rattling noise when the animal moves, thereby warning other animals of its approach; the number of bones contained in the rattle varies according to its age, one being added every year, from which it appears to live about twelve years, as snakes are sometimes killed with that number of bones in the rattle; when about to strike an animal it coils itself up like the contraction, (&) to enable it to dart forward its head with greater rapidity, and without any part of its body touching the ground, except the tail, on which it supports itself during the time. This reptile is becoming less and less numerous, as none are allowed to escape when once observed. They are usually found in pairs, and often among the growing corn. A neighbour of ours was once bitten with one on which he had accidentally trodden. He killed it immediately afterwards, and then hastened to the nearest house, but before he could reach it he was obliged to hollow to make the occupiers know what was his misfortune, as he felt his tongue and limbs beginning to grow stiff; the antidote was immediately administered, but not before he had become insensible; he however, recovered. When an individual attacks these reptiles he should be cautious how he approaches them when in their favourite coiled position. When they are extended at length on the ground, they may be approached with safety, as they are then not able to dart forward their heads as they do when they attempt to inflict a wound.

Insects are likewise numerous in America, and many of them of a larger size than any to be met with in England. There is a species of ant found on the prairies, about half the size of a working bee. In traversing these grounds, particularly in summer, a person will naturally feel inclined to rest himself occasionally, and may probably select for himself, as a seat, some little hillock, of which there are many. If he does, however, I will venture to assert he will be caught trespassing, and have to pay the smart too.

The butterflies in America are really splendid, nothing can surpass them in design, depth of colouring, or in the delicacy with which their finely powdered wings are finished. I have sometimes observed in very hot weather, when I happened to throw to the door a little greasy or soapy water, that the place thus moistened has been covered in a few minutes with butterflies of the richest and most brilliant dress. All the hues that the prism can elicit from the "parent of colours," have been there manifested, and that with such a beautifully variegated combination, as to render imitation utterly impracticable.

The plan proposed in this narrative requires that mention be made only of such objects as would come under the notice of common observers, whereby a tolerably correct idea of the general state of the country may be obtained. I cannot however close these succinct observations on insects, without noticing one which flies about during the evenings in summer, and emits a light considerably brighter than that of the glow worm. When I first beheld it, I was not aware of its existence. It was one evening as husband and I were returning from the chapel, on a road that was principally through an uncultivated piece of wooded land. As we were passing along, we observed in many places what we took to be sparks of fire dancing about most mysteriously. Our curiosity was excited not a little, but not knowing what to think, we dared not approach them, for fear they were connected with something super-human. Superstition certainly got hold of us, and we hastened home imagining some strange catastrophe was about to occur. On reaching home we found a neighbour waiting our arrival, to whom we related what we had witnessed. He smiled at our simplicity, and told us they were light bugs, the name they are known by in Illinois; fire-flies I believe is a more general term, which gave us no small satisfaction, as we had been much disturbed to know what such a prodigy could imply.

A few pages back I attempted to describe the appearance of a winter night. I may now be allowed to make a few remarks on the peculiarities of a night in summer. As our situation in America is about fourteen degrees further south than Yorkshire, I scarcely need say that the shortest summer night there is longer than the shortest in England by two or three hours. In this country, as the shades of twilight gradually usher in the more sombre aspect of night, a delightful silence seems to repose on the bosom of nature. Hence Milton: "Now came still evening on and twilight grey," &c. The reverse of this is nearer the truth in Illinois. It would be a burlesque on language for any one during a night in summer, to repeat Grey's admired line,—"All the air a solemn stillness holds." I have already stated that owls are very numerous, they are also very noisy during the night. There is another bird, however, that outdoes them in this respect. It is about the size of a lark, and has a loud voice, but only three notes, which it keeps continually repeating. It thus appears to keep crying: "Whip away," or "Whip poor Will," as some will have it. Hence one or other of these terms is the name of the bird, which I believe is common through all North America. Unceasing as are the noises made by these nocturnal performers, there is a species of frog, known as the bull-frog, whose voice completely drowns the preceding; it abounds in small creeks and ponds, of which there are many in some districts, though none near our farm. The moment this animal observes darkness approaching, it begins its tremendous croakings, which, as its name suggests, are more like the bellowing of a bull than the voice of a frog.

Other animals might be mentioned with propriety, as being peculiar to that country, as the mink, the opossum, and the raccoon; but as these are fully described in works on natural history, I forbear to enlarge, after I have related the following little incident. The foot-print of the last-named animal is precisely like that which a little child, just able to walk, would make. There is the rounded heel, the hollow under the rise of the metatarsus, the toes, and toe nails, as exactly delineated as if it had been actually made with the foot of a child. This impression we observed before we knew anything about it. My husband's curiosity led him to trace it across a ploughed field, as he really thought these prints had been made either by fairies or the diminutive offspring of some concealed Indians, and was a long time before he could be persuaded they were made by a quadruped. If the reader consults a volume on natural history, he will find this animal classed among the plantigrada, which will partly account for the above circumstance.

The continuation of my narrative presents my partner recovered from his lameness, and busy thrashing our wheat in the open air: we had a small barn, but as the ground is almost as hard as a boarded floor at the season I am now speaking of, the corn is often thrashed in the open air. Many farmers thrash as soon as harvest is over, and, without winnowing it, place it on a large heap, and cover it with a thick coat of straw and another of earth, as farmers preserve potatoes in England. In this state it will keep very well for several months if required. As the cattle lie out all the year round, the straw is of no use, they therefore burn it out of their way. The time had not yet arrived for us to practise this system of preserving corn; we wanted the full worth of our wheat, and that as soon as we could get. As we had no winnowing machine we were obliged to winnow with the wind, which, though a troublesome method, is frequently practised in Illinois, for the same reason as that which induced us to practise it on this occasion. The farmers in that country are much troubled with a weed that grows amongst the wheat, and of which it is next to an impossibility to clear it. This was the first time we had anything to do with it. Its appearance when growing can scarcely be distinguished from wheat till it begins to ear; on this account it is called 'cheat,' and not undeservedly, as it sometimes stands on the ground as abundant as the crop itself, and yet it is so valueless, that even the poultry will not eat it. I have not seen anything in England that resembles it more nearly than the weeds termed by Yorkshire farmers droke and darnel. It is more like the former than the latter.

Having thrashed and winnowed our wheat in the manner above described, our next consideration was how we were to sell it. The produce of the three acres might be about eighty bushels, one-fourth of which was but imperfectly cleared of cheat, and was therefore unsaleable. We had only five sacks, which we had taken with us from England, but these even we did not require, as we subsequently learnt the store-keepers were accustomed to furnish the settlers with bags for their corn. My husband took a specimen of wheat, which as it had been sown too sparingly on the ground was a fine sample. Mr. Varley offered half a dollar per bushel in money, or a few cents more in barter. We borrowed a waggon and a yoke of oxen of one of our neighbours, and carried to the store fifty bushels. The first thing we did was to settle our meal account; we next bought two pairs of shoes for self and husband, which by this time we wanted as we did other articles of apparel, which we knew we could conveniently procure. The truth is, we had intended to have a little more clothing, but finding the prices so extravagant, we felt compelled to abandon that intention. For a yard of common printed calico, they asked half a dollar, or a bushel of wheat, and proportionate prices for other goods. We gave ten bushels of wheat for the shoes. I may just remark that the prices are considerably lower at the present time for all kinds of wearables than they were then. Our next purchase was a plough, bought in hopes that we should, at some time, have cattle to draw it, as we were tired of the hoeing system. We also bought two tin milk bowls; these and the plough cost about twenty bushels. We obtained further a few pounds of coffee, and a little meal; the coffee cost us at the rate of a dollar for four pounds; and thus we laid out the greater part of our first crop of wheat. We had only reserved about twenty bushels for seed, besides a quantity imperfectly cleared of cheat, which was unfit either for sale or making bread. On balancing our account with Mr. Varley, we found we had to take about five dollars, which we received in paper money, specie being exceedingly scarce in Illinois.

The interval between this time and the latter part of September, was spent in further clearing the field which we had before fenced somewhat more than half round. Our Indian corn was likely to be a failing crop, partly because it had been sown late, and partly for want of a plough it had been but imperfectly cultivated. The autumnal rains had now begun to fall, and while other people's corn was ripe, a great part of ours was quite green, and not likely to ripen before the frosts. The little that was ready, we cut, and made it into small stacks, to be ready for seed the ensuing spring. October arrived; it was the season for sowing wheat, and we were little better prepared than we had been the preceding spring; for although we had a plough we had no team. We could readily have hired one had we possessed the means. Five or six dollars were all the money we had, and we fully purposed to buy a pig or two with them, as we had been some weeks without any animal food, except a few fowls for which we had bartered one of our china tea-cups. Our inability to raise a team and sow our wheat, was a source of very great anxiety. The hoeing system had answered so indifferently that we felt determined, if possible to have it ploughed. We knew a Mr. Knowles who ploughed for hire; his house was about two miles from ours. My husband waited upon him and offered him one-fifth of the produce of eight acres for ploughing and harrowing it. Reward, it is said, sweetens labour: of this Mr. Knowles was conscious; but the idea of waiting for the reward till the ensuing harvest did not suit his genius: in short, he declined undertaking the work on any such terms. My husband was coming away almost in despair; but happening to look at his watch, Mr. Knowles accosted him in a tone of surprise that he should want any one to work on credit while he possessed such a watch as that, telling him at the same time, that he would plough and harrow the whole eight acres for it. I need scarcely say they immediately agreed, as the watch had been bought in England a year or two before for something less than a sovereign. We were thus relieved from our distressing anxiety, and got the wheat sown as conveniently as we could possibly wish.

This acquaintance with Mr. Knowles led to a further bargain between him and my husband for three young pigs just taken in from the range; for which we paid him the small sum of three dollars. They were scarcely fat enough to kill; we therefore gave them a little unsaleable wheat which fed them very rapidly, so that in about a month's time they became nice pork, weighing between nine and ten stones each. By this time our little stock of cattle required to be fed daily with Indian corn, part of which was uncut, and what is worse some of it was unripe. That which had ripened was excellent fodder, the greater part of which we had cut: the little that remained in the field, being ripe, suffered no harm; whereas, the last sown, not ripening before the frosts came on, was much injured, the cattle would scarcely touch it. There is nothing peculiar in this: water, it is well known, expands when it is frozen. Hence, all sorts of succulent plants or soft grain, having their vessels filled with a watery or juicy substance, must of necessity, when frozen, experience a disarrangement of their parts, and have their vascular structure destroyed, and consequently be liable to putrefaction and mould.

In the various transactions I have had to enumerate, I have overlooked our potato crop which was abundant; for although we had only planted half a rood, we had more than sufficient for our own use. The reader must be aware that no manure is used for any thing that is grown: the land is as fat as nature requires, and tillage would, in its present state, rather injure it than otherwise. We had not sown any turnips this year; they are generally sown in July, immediately after the wheat crop is reaped, and often on the land on which it has grown. In all probability we should have endeavoured to sow some, had not my husband at this time been an invalid.

The first Sunday in November was the anniversary of our landing in America, for we have now gone through the principal events of our first year's residence in that country. It was further distinguished as being the day on which the yearly feast is held at the little village where we had lived in England. This circumstance, trifling as it is, had a tendency to bring to our recollection in a most vivid manner, bygone associations and endearments, the value of which we only discovered when they were lost. Does the reader ask for an explanation? Let him consider for a while our condition; and if experience has taught him anything of the nature of those feelings which the love of one's country inspires; if he knows even what emotions are kindled by being removed from old and congenial attachments, he will perceive we had reasons for being sad on the occasion here referred to. The difficulties and privations we had already endured were not forgotten. The tattered appearance of our children's clothes, compared with what they had worn in England, made an impression on our minds, which even patient endurance could not resist. We were again on the eve of a hard winter with less warm clothing to meet it, than we had the preceding winter by the wear of a twelvemonth. This was one of the gloomy days in our history. The previous winter we had been prevented from attending religious worship on account of distance, we were now prevented from another cause,—want of decent clothing. It was on this occasion that we perceived something more than poetry in the lines of Cowper:

"When I think of my own native land,
In a moment I seem to be there;
But alas! recollection at hand
Soon hurries me back to despair."

There was however one cheering consideration: in all respects except clothing, we were better situated than we had been the foregoing season. We had four acres more of wheat sown this year than the year before; we were now in possession of a plough; our cattle had likewise increased in value; the cow had calved again, and the former calf had grown a fine-looking heifer, we therefore saw, after all, we were gaining ground.

A True Picture of Emigration

In accordance with my pretensions, I ought here to state that both I and husband had the ague very bad this month; happily not both at the same time. This complaint is too well known to require any description of it from me. It generally attacks new settlers at the end of their first summer, and, even afterwards. At the fall of the leaf it is by no means an uncommon complaint. As land becomes better cultivated and drained, this disease is less frequent. At the present time, notwithstanding its prevalence in autumn, it rarely proves fatal, except in instances where the constitution has manifested previous symptoms of decline, and like a withered leaf is ready to be blown down by the first fresh breeze that blows. The inhabitants have various specifics, real and imaginary: a weak infusion of common pot-herbs drunk hot appears to be as efficacious as anything. When the patient ceases to shake, the ague is said to be broken, and unless fever ensue, as it sometimes happens, he is in a short time quite well.

After we had recovered, for a while nothing occurred worthy of note. As, in the winter previous, our chief employment consisted in attending to the cattle, preparing firewood, and splitting rails. As before, our cattle remained out day and night, generally resorting, during the latter, to some sheltered situation. About Christmas, a person with whom we had had several interviews, named Mr. Vanderoozen,[1] came to our house and wished us to buy two young steers and a milch cow. We replied we could not purchase them for want of money. "That reason," said he, "shall not prevent you: I am going to keep a shop at St. Louis, and shall often have to come up into the country, you may pay for them when it is convenient, meanwhile I shall expect interest for my money." At the time I am now speaking of, the usual interest paid for the loan of money was twenty-five per cent per annum. It has since very properly declined to twelve per cent. Having considered Mr. Vanderoozen's proposal, we felt inclined to accept it; the only impediment was in the failure of our Indian corn crop. By using the remainder of our unsaleable wheat, however, we presumed we should be able to winter them, and felt assured that when spring arrived they would be able to do well, and greatly add to our advantages. The bargain was accordingly

[1] Garret Van Dusen, a resident of Pike County from 1821 to about 1850. He was a Kentuckian and an early commissioner of Pike County, a farmer, and a stock trader. Nothing further is known concerning him, or his family. Information supplied by Jess M. Thompson.

struck: my husband gave him a promissory note for thirty dollars, with interest for the same at the same rate. We thus appeared to have increased our possessions, and endeavoured to brave our privations and the severity of the weather as well as we could. We were obliged, nevertheless, to economize our winter fodder, which was seen in the condition of our cattle; by degrees they began to lose their flesh, a circumstance which made us doubly anxious for the return of spring.

After much anxiety and unceasing diligence to preserve the health of our stock, the first of March arrived. In a fortnight more we expected there would be plenty of fresh grass in the wilds, and we consequently looked forward to the time with pleasure, little anticipating how sudden a check to our satisfaction we were about to receive. On the third of March, who should darken our door but Mr. Vanderoozen, who had, as he expressed himself, called upon us for the money we owed him; that is to say, the thirty dollars we had agreed to give him for the steers and cow. Thunderstruck at a request so unexpected and unreasonable, we expostulated with him on the terms of the agreement, and explained our inability to answer his demands. Unfortunately the note we had given him contained no intimation as to the time our creditor had allowed us. All our expostulations were unheeded; he withdrew, assuring us he would immediately make use of the means the law allowed him for obtaining his money. He was as good as his word; the following day an Esquire* waited upon us with a writ, which allowed us only a few days to prepare for its demands. Our only method of preventing the seizure of our property forthwith was either to replevin or pay the money. The idea of a law-suit was neither adapted to our feelings nor circumstances; but how were we to raise the money? It is not so easy to raise money ✓ for cattle in Illinois as in England; besides ours were at that time looking ill, and would consequently be undervalued. Should an execution be issued our cattle would be driven to the appointed place for the sale of distrained goods, and sold by auction, be the price what it would. In all probability our whole stock thus sacrificed would be inadequate to the debt and expenses, which would place our very land in jeopardy. Now it was that we regretted having bought them on credit. Remorse the most pungent preyed on our heart-strings. The emaciated appearance

*A legal officer, so named, whose duties embody both those of attorney and policeman.

of our cattle condemned our cupidity, and upbraided us with all our contrivances to economize their provender.

Meanwhile the time approached for us to answer the demands of our creditor, or submit to the process of the law. We had only one plan in view which appeared at all likely to avert the threatened calamity. Our friend Mr. B. had been privy to this speculation, and had commended our resolves. He had plenty of money in his possession, as he had made no heavy purchases since he obtained the remittance, and he was naturally thrifty. Two days before the time expired, my husband went to him and explained the conduct of Vanderoozen, requesting him either to buy some of our cattle or lend the money, for which ample interest should be paid. It is unpleasant to record this part of the conduct of our countryman, yet truth demands that I should say he refused to do either, alleging that he did not want any more cattle, nor did he like to lend his money. This refusal rendered our wretchedness complete. After my husband had heard his denial his feelings were too heavily laden for him to urge any more. He came home melancholy enough, without having made any reply to his refusal. I shall never forget his return that evening. During his

absence my mind had been in a state of vac-
illation between hope and fear; but the moment I saw his countenance hope entirely
fled. What kind of a night we experienced,
those alone can conceive who have struggled
earnestly and perseveringly with adversity
without success. In vain did we extend our
languid limbs on our homely couch. Spirits
so disordered as ours, were beyond the powers of sleep to lull into forgetfulness. The
entire labours of a twelve month were
doomed to disappear. On other occasions
when my spirits had been depressed, I had
laid my cause before the Supreme Ruler, and
found relief; but at this time I felt no disposition to look upward. We seemed despised
and forsaken by all. In this state of mind
we continued until morning, when a knock
was heard at the door, to which my husband
attended. Will the reader here believe my
story? Shall I not rather be charged with
fabrication? I can, however, tax no one with
incredulity, inasmuch as I doubted my husband's assertion myself, when, returning
from the door, he told me that Mr. B. had
brought us the money, and gone away saying he could not rest any longer without
lending it.

This account I am aware has too much of
the air of fiction, appears too nearly allied to

the marvellous to obtain general credit. It might have been suppressed, but as I am prompted to regard it as an instance of the over-ruling power of that being "who maketh the wrath of man to praise him," I deem it to be my duty to record it as it occurred, and where it is now placed. The story is now easy to conclude: the following day, to the surprise of our creditor, we paid the money, and thereby put an end to the proceedings. We had no sooner settled this affair than we turned out our cattle into the woods, having previously marked them on the right ear. The sugar trees were now ready for tapping, and as we were anxious to pay Mr. B. as soon as we could, we resolved to make the best of them, especially as sugar is an article for which money can be easily obtained. We made incisions into a great many trees, and shortly had our large kettles boiling down the liquor; the greatest difficulty we experienced arose from an insufficiency of troughs to place at the bottom of the trees. We were obliged to cork up the holes of the greater part to prevent the liquor from wasting, while the rest alternately were running into the troughs. Notwithstanding this hindrance, we made at least three hundred and fifty pounds of sugar, which enabled us to return our friend fifteen dollars, half the sum we had borrowed. For the loan of the remainder my husband agreed to work for him five days in the year, till we could return it. The sugar this year did exceedingly well; for besides raising the above sum, we exchanged about forty pounds of it for a sow and a litter of pigs, which we kept near home till they knew the premises, and afterwards allowed them to run at large till autumn.

Thus, the reader will perceive our circumstances kept improving, as we had now two milch cows, two steers almost ready for the yoke, one young heifer, a calf, a fine young mare, and the family of pigs just named. In agricultural pursuits every season presents its peculiar task to the husbandman, and situated as we were that task was not a small one; the season for sowing Indian corn had again arrived, and again we were unprepared with a team. In the whole round of our agricultural labours nothing so much perplexed us as the sowing of our corn; we had only four acres this spring as we had sown eight with wheat, and all our other land was unbroken up; having no fixed plan in view and not knowing what means to adopt to get in the seed, we were agreeably surprised one morning to behold a person in the field busy ploughing; this was Mr. Burns,

the person named on a previous occasion,
with whom we had formed an intimacy, or
rather a friendship, which up to the time
I am writing has only increased in degree
and in value; in any country such a person as he would be valuable as a friend,
but in the thinly inhabited regions of the
"far west," his worth cannot be fully set
forth; his kindness towards us at this time
is, however, a specimen; he and his wife had
been at our house the previous week, and
perceiving our coming difficulty, gave us the
above seasonable boon; we thus saw the
whole of the twelve acres systematically
sown: the wheat was a fine thriving crop, we
therefore began to feel ourselves more composed, and to use a good old English phrase
"more at home."

Hitherto we had no garden, my husband
therefore dug up about a rood of fine dry
land, and fenced it round with brush-work
after the Yorkshire style of dead fencing; the
greater part of it we planted with potatoes,
and the rest with other kinds of vegetables,
obtaining the seeds and plants from older settlers; before our wheat crop was ripe we had
finished the fence round the new field, and
rooted up the greater part of the underwood
growing thereon; most of the stronger timbers we allowed to stand, having previously

cut the bark on the trunk to prevent their growing; the rest we decapitated, and kindled fires round their stems to burn them away; this employment and the attending to our cattle, employed the whole of our time till the wheat harvest, and I assure the reader we were not idle: at the usual time, about the end of June, we began to cut our wheat, retaining the old sickles which we had borrowed the year before.

Mr. B., who by this time had got married, intimated to my husband that he should require his help a few days, according to agreement for the loan of the money. As our corn[1] was ripe and in that state requiring immediate attention, my husband tried to mow some of it down with an old scythe we had taken with us from England; this was tremendous heavy work, as the crop was abundant. Scarcely anything that occurred to us, taking into account the comparative insignificance of the article was more vexatious than the want of something with which to sharpen our tools; I have heard my husband say he would cheerfully work a fortnight for a good Yorkshire scythe-stone and a wrag-whetstone; the stone we used for that purpose was a very poor one, being a

[1] The allusion is to the wheat crop, not the Indian corn.

sort of flinty limestone which we found on the land; subsequently we met with another, much superior, apparently a piece of sandstone, but so fine as not to appear granular. Not knowing how soon Mr. B. might require assistance, my husband continued mowing, while I and our son used the sickles, thus cutting down in the whole about an acre per day, leaving from necessity the mown part abroad on the ground, to be taken up and bound into sheaves afterwards; we had finished within a day's work before Mr. B. required my husband's help; my son and I, therefore, were left to cut the remainder, which we did in two days; we then proceeded to take up the remainder and bind it into sheaves.

While thus employed a circumstance occurred, which at the time was quite alarming; the excessive heat of the sun, added to another cause which the reader will understand when he is told that the September following I was confined of twins, made me feel much fatigued, and caused me to rest on a sheaf several times during a day: one time while thus seated, a large full-grown rattlesnake crawled idly out of the sheaf on which I was sitting; horrified with the sight, and scarcely knowing what I did, I seized my rake and struck it on the head several times, whereby it soon died; this event, although not of two minutes continuance, proved a lasting warning to me to be cautious, and even to this moment I never call it to mind without feelings of peculiar uneasiness; the sudden start made me so feeble for a while that I could not proceed with my labour. I however took care not to rest on a sheaf: shortly after, as we expected, we saw another, apparently in search of its mate, which I destroyed in like manner; when they were dead, my children took them home as trophies of triumph, to shew to their father in the evening, who at the recital of my story, joined with me in thanks to Heaven for preservation in such imminent danger.

The following day my husband being with us, we expected to get through this part of our business in the harvest field; having nearly finished before dinner he took one of the children with him, during the noontide recess, to look at the fires kindled around the trees as before explained; trivial as this circumstance appears, its consequences were dreadful; by some means the little child set fire to her dress, which frightened her so much that she immediately ran among the sheaves which were lying on the ground just at hand; my husband, all intent to the situation of the girl, did not perceive that the

sheaves were on a blaze till he had put out
the fire on the child's clothes; he immediately gave an alarm, I ran to the door, but
who can depict my feelings when I beheld
our fine crop of wheat, the greatest treasure
we possessed, and that on which our hopes
principally rested for the speedy supplying
of our various pressing necessities, blazing
and cracking with prodigious vehemence. I
need scarcely say every nerve was strained
to its utmost to extinguish it; a small stream
or branch ran at a short distance; guided by
the first impulse of reason, we hastened
thither immediately with the first vessels we
could lay hold of, but although we ran both
ways to the utmost of our strength, the
flames spread further and further, we soon
perceived this method would be unavailing.

Here was a trial for all our powers, mental
and bodily. To extinguish the flames was impossible, the straw was so dry, and the heat
became intolerable. There is generally a
time for consideration, and a time for active
labour. It was not so here, while we were
considering our property was burning, and
that with a speed indescribable. Directed,
I cannot but think by Providence, we hit
upon a plan which promised success. This
was to make a separation between the side
that was on fire and the other. It was no

sooner conceived than we began to effect it. We removed the sheaves with all the expedition in our power to cut off all communication with the bulk of the crop. As much as we were able, we removed to the further side: but to save the side in question, we were obliged, from want of strength, to throw some to the devouring element. A division was at last happily completed, and the vacant space was too wide for the flames to cross, although in some instances they appeared to bound from one sheaf to another. Want of additional fuel alone extinguished the flames. Not a particle of combustible matter was left unconsumed where the fire had raged; it was one entire plain of smouldering black ashes, we thus lost about an acre and had it not been for one apparently insignificant circumstance, the whole would have been inevitably lost: the fire prevailed only where the wheat had been mown, had it once obtained possession of the long shorn stubble, all our attempts would have ended in woeful disappointment, as it was, in our situation the loss was no trifle, yet the uppermost emotions in our minds were rather those of pleasure than of pain, and with sufficient reason; we had seven acres remaining, whereas, half-an-hour before we had feared it was all lost.

A True Picture of Emigration

After we were fully assured the fire was out we sat down and wept; but our tears were, if I may use the expression, tears of thanksgiving. We called to mind the various difficulties through which we had successfully struggled, and we looked upon this as another pledge of ultimate success. We may indeed date the commencement of a moderately comfortable existence from this occurrence. The wheat was very fine indeed, but, as before, mixed with cheat; we had about two hundred and twenty bushels, forty of which were unsaleable on account of this troublesome weed. It is unnecessary to trouble the reader with all the particulars of our future proceedings, as it would be a repetition of customs and exercises I have already described.

Having been tolerably minute in detailing our various transactions and difficulties for nearly two years, till, as the reader has seen, our narrative begins to wear a brighter aspect, it will now be sufficient for the purpose here contemplated to give a sketch of the most prominent features of our future proceedings: we purchased several articles of wearing apparel with our wheat, paid off a small account for salt, and obtained gearing for a yoke of oxen, purposing to plough our land this fall with young oxen bought of

Vanderoozen, besides supplying our immediate wants in clothing, which we did only sparingly, we were enabled to leave in the hands of Mr. Varley, forty dollars, for which he agreed to pay us interest if we allowed it to remain in his hands six months. We should have paid Mr. B., but as my husband had worked for him five days we considered it as our own to the end of the year. There was one trivial advantage in our wheat taking fire; we intended to sow an acre of turnips, and this part having no stubble on, it was the part we selected as being the most ready for the plough. We engaged Mr. Knowles to plough the land, giving him three dollars for his labour. We made a further arrangement with this gentleman to plough our late enclosed field with his prairie plough at the fall of the leaf, and in the meantime we endeavoured to cleanse of roots the part unfinished; it is exceedingly heavy work to break up the land with this plough, requiring four yoke of oxen to draw it; we paid him four dollars per acre for doing it. According to our intentions we yoked our two young steers to plough the land for wheat, our kind friend Mr. Burns, voluntarily spending the first day with us to give my husband a little instruction relative to driving and gearing them. They served our purpose very well, which gave us unspeakable pleasure and satisfaction; nor did we value this advantage unduly, considering the anxieties we had felt on former occasions for want of it.

During the summer, our cattle throve very well; the cow we purchased of Vanderoozen had calved again, and our other cow and the heifer were both near calving. Cattle begin to breed much sooner in Illinois than in England; this may partly be attributed to the climate, which causes them to grow to maturity sooner in that country than in this; another reason is, being allowed to range at large during summer, where cattle of both sexes abound, the farmer has no means of preventing this circumstance. We have before noticed that it is customary for the farmers to kill as many of their hogs and horned cattle at the fall of the leaf, as they do not intend to keep over winter. They are often in excellent condition when they come up, not exactly what an English butcher would call prime beef. Hogs are scarcely fat enough to be killed, they are usually served with a little corn a few weeks after they have ceased to range, and thereby become very good bacon. Fat cattle is a source of income to the farmer, from which we had hitherto derived no benefit, nor at present had we aught but our pigs which we purposed to kill, and of these we had not sufficient to offer any for sale, as we wished to keep some over winter to breed the ensuing season.

The interval between this and the following autumn contained nothing deserving particular note. We sowed the new field with Indian corn. It was readily ploughed, having been broken up as before stated the previous fall, and exposed to the frosts during winter. The weather was too hot during the sugar season, which prevented our realizing as much from that article as we had done the foregoing year. It however enabled us to pay Mr. B. the money we owed him without entirely exhausting our little fund of reserve. After reaping our wheat this season, our neighbour, Mr. Paddock, expressed a wish to sell us the pre-emption right to his land. Like many persons in Illinois, this individual wanted industry, as he rarely worked more than half of his time. He had been more than three years on it, and would consequently lose all right to it in a short time, unless he paid the government demands—one hundred dollars, before the period expired. Notwithstanding his love of ease, he was not without the means to pay for it; but preferred, as he said, a change, and intended to migrate to another unimproved situation, and there spend four years, or

perhaps longer, if no one thwarted his interests. As his land was contiguous to ours
on one point, we thought it would be a good
speculation to purchase it, especially as the
price he set upon the improvement was very
moderate. He had fourteen or fifteen acres
broken up, besides the house, which was a
tolerably good one of the kind. He valued
his labour at fifty dollars, and offered to receive payment in either cattle or wheat at a
fair price. We hesitated a long time before
we decided, foreseeing that unless we paid
for it at the land office the succeeding spring,
we should be liable to lose it. We however
finally determined to have it, and as our cattle had again done well, we gave him a good
cow, a heifer, and seventy bushels of wheat,
which he disposed of at his pleasure. Mr.
Paddock, after this, speedily vacated the
house, wishing to erect another before the
frosts should set in. The only instrument we
received as a proof of the bargain, was the
pre-emption certificate, which Mr. Paddock
had obtained from the recording office, en-
dorsed with his name, ratifying the agreement. This was, however, sufficient testi-
mony. One day shortly after, a Mr. Carr,
hearing that Paddock had removed, came to
his late possessions and found my husband
repairing a fence. He seemed to interest

himself very much in the situation, and asked
several questions respecting the pre-emption
right, &c. His questions were evaded as
well as civility would allow. They, however,
served to premonish us that Mr. Carr had
some sinister plans affecting that property,
and we knew that if he took possession of the
house it would be a very troublesome affair.

Though these considerations were based
only on conjecture, the disreputable character of Mr. Carr, added to his suspicious manner, gave them much of the force of reality.
Perplexed with these ideas, we scarcely knew
what course to adopt. At one time we
thought it advisable to set fire to the house
and burn it down; then again we wished it
not to be known that we feared for its safety;
besides it would be very useful to keep farming implements in, or it would serve as a pig-
gery or sheep cot if we wanted. We would
have gone immediately to the land office and
paid for it, if we had possessed sufficient
money; we expected, however, our sugar-
orchard would make up the deficit the following spring. To quiet our apprehensions
in the present instance, our only feasible
method appeared to be, that we should take
possession of the house ourselves. But here
was another obstacle: it was impossible that
we could leave our present establishment, on

account of our cattle and dairy being kept
there. We found we should be obliged to di-
vide our family, and have one part at Mr.
Paddock's late residence and the other at our
own. My husband would have cheerfully
gone to the newly purchased situation, had
not his presence and services at home among
the cattle been indispensable. It evidently
therefore became my duty to undertake the
unpleasant task of leaving home, to occupy
a house which we feared an unprincipled
intruder wished to inhabit. I had however
grown accustomed to hardships even more
severe than this. I took with me our two
youngest children, something with which to
warm our food, and a bed. As the house was
only half a mile from our own, I frequently saw
the other parts of the family during the day;
but the nights seemed dreary and long. For
a few days nobody came near us, and I would
have gladly hoped our fears were groundless.

They eventually proved but too true, as
the following account sufficiently manifests.
One afternoon, after I had been living in this
manner about a week, a person drove a
clumsy waggon to the door, containing a
little furniture, a woman, and two children.
I shut the door, and endeavoured to fasten
the latch, there being no lock. But the man,
who I afterwards learnt was Mr. Carr,

quickly forced it open, and bidding his wife walk in, said to her,—well, my dear, this is our house: how do you like it? without seeming to notice me in the least. He then carried in their furniture, and then, for the first time, found leisure to speak to me. He told me they could do without my company pretty well, and wished me to be a good neighbour and go home. There were two rooms; I took my bed and other articles into the other which was unoccupied, and felt very anxious to see my husband. He came in the evening, and saw what had occurred. Mr. Carr held up a paper as a defiance, and told him that it was the certificate obtained at the land office, Quincy, as a title to the estate. We were assured he could not have purchased it legally; and we even doubted that he had paid for it at all. When my husband attempted to enter the house, Mr. Carr shut the door, and resisted with all his force; but being inferior in strength, admittance was obtained. On perceiving us engaged in a whispered conversation, he intimated that if we intended to spend the night in his house, he would go and make use of ours, to which we made no reply.

The result of our deliberation was, that my husband should ride over to Quincy, a distance of fifty miles, take the pre-emption certificate with him, and ascertain whether through perjury he had purchased the land. Shortly after, my husband went home, and on his arrival found Mr. Carr, whom, as I afterwards learnt, he quickly made scamper. Next morning he called with a quantity of provisions, and took leave of me for his journey, which would take him three days; no one but myself knowing the purport of his leaving home. It was most uncomfortable for me to be thus left with only two little children under the same roof with a family whose sentiments towards me were the most unfriendly imaginable, and whose character stood assuredly not very high for probity. In the fullest and worst sense of the word, I was a prisoner, not daring to leave the room, and exposed to the jeers and taunts of a malicious man who left no means untried, short of personal violence, to expel me from the house; telling me my husband had sent me there to get rid of me, with a thousand other fabricated and tantalizing remarks.

The third day, which was the Sabbath, having sent for my Bible, I endeavoured to solace myself by perusing its sacred pages. This made him more furious than ever; uttering the most blasphemous imprecations, he vowed 'he would be both rid of me, and my cursed religion before long.' About ten

in the forenoon, two or three of his friends
came to see him, who, finding or knowing
how matters stood, assisted him in his attempts to deride me. I really thought I now
must surrender, and had it not been for the
man's wife, who checked their scorn, I am
apt to think I should have been obliged to
withdraw. After dinner my situation took a
favourable turn. By some means or other
many of our neighbours having learnt where I
was and on what account, came to the house
to see me. For a while my keeper refused admittance to all, till by and by there was quite
a crowd at the door. I conversed with some
females whom I knew through an aperture in
the wall, which served for a window; and as
many of them wished to enter, a number of
men favourable to our interests told my disappointed persecutor if he did not allow the
females to visit me, they would convince him
he was no master. Awed by this declaration,
he opened the door and the house was immediately filled, Mr. Carr and his party appear-
ing completely nonplused. And, so strangely
had matters changed, that religious worship
was held in the place that evening, suggested √
by a few pious friends, who seeing my Bible,
had thought it their duty to propose it.

This was too much for Mr. Carr; he entirely
left the premises during service. Towards

nightfall the arrival of my husband was announced, who was much surprised to find me so well attended. He told Mr. Carr, in the presence of the persons congregated, where he had been, and how his perjury was detected. He likewise gave him to understand that he would probably find he had acted imprudently as well as wickedly. But the most agreeable part of the intelligence to me was, that there was no necessity for me to remain any longer in the house. I therefore very willingly left it and accompanied my husband to our own habitation, having first thanked my friends for their kind interference and regard. The sum of the particulars is, that Mr. Carr had paid for the land, having previously sworn there was no improvement on it; although a pre-emption certificate had been obtained at the recording office, Pittsfield. Of course the purchase was illegal, and Carr liable to a heavy penalty. The following morning, we learnt our firmness had acted powerfully on the mind of our opponent, as his wife called upon us to say that her husband was willing to make a compromise, and would either pay us for our claims on the estate or sell his certificate. This proposal required some consideration; we therefore gave her no definite answer, but told her if her husband wished to have an interview with us, notwithstanding his base conduct, we would treat him with civility. In the meantime, we considered it best to sell our pre-emption right, if he would produce the money, as we knew we could not buy his certificate at that time. In a day or two our opponent waited upon us wishing to have us pacified, as he knew he had acted criminally. We told him we would allow him peaceable possession on the payment of eighty dollars for the improvement, which he agreed to pay, and shortly afterwards the affair was settled, eventually to our advantage, though it cost us some anguish of mind. The peculiarity of the American law respecting the purchase of land, although framed originally with the view of assisting new settlers, is not infrequently a source of strife; at the present time there are many persons who have cultivated land for numbers of years, without paying anything for it; and there is no means of knowing, except by applying at the land office. Should, however, this counsel escape them, some one would be sure to go and purchase it, or even reap some of the corn when ripe, the original cultivator having no legal power to prevent them.

There is another peculiar clause in these laws respecting original rights; I refer to the erection of mills. I have before stated that water mills are the most common; the reason of this is obvious. When, therefore, a person purchases a section of land, it is his interest to examine whether there is a mill-seat on any stream that may run through it; if there is, he must apply to the recording office to have it "condemned." This prevents any other person from erecting a mill within a certain distance; I believe two miles. If, however, after two years the site is not built upon, the owner loses his prerogative. This law caused a piece of knavery to be practised upon us; the branch running through our farm had a very good site on it for a mill; some of our friends advised us to get it condemned; we did so, rather with a view of selling the site than of erecting a mill ourselves. About a year and a half afterwards, a person called upon us named Phillips, the identical person at whose house we had spent the first night in Illinois, with a view of buying it; after a little deliberation we sold it to him for one hundred and fifty dollars; not having cash by him, as he said, he would call again in a short time and pay for it; my husband desired to have the agreement drawn up in a proper form, but as Mr. Phillips averred his word was his surest bond it was omitted. He, however, proved a villain and the tool of another; for, by continuing to evade payment by specious promises, he contrived to keep us in suspense till the two years had expired, when another person, his employer, immediately began to erect a mill very near our farm; thus were we defrauded of our right to be millers.

Perhaps the foregoing incidents may place the inhabitants of the western world in an unfavourable light; as a few remarks appear, therefore, to be called for, not indeed to unsay what has been said, "facts are stubborn things;" but to serve as an explanation of the occurrences above narrated. It must be borne in mind that ignorance is a predominant feature in their character, indeed it can hardly be otherwise; not that they are less gifted than the Europeans from whom they have originated, but because their opportunities for cultivating their minds are so limited; besides, their pursuits and manner of living do not require much intellectual training; a really learned man would be in solitude amongst them, and his talents, like the vaticinating genius of an ill-fated Cassandra, unappreciated or unperceived. The American government has, indeed, very humanely appropriated a certain portion of land for the maintenance of schools through the length and breadth of the country; this endowment naturally varies with the value of the land.

A True Picture of Emigration

In the States where the land has become more valuable by an increased population, it is pretty good, and consequently commands men of talent; but in the remoter regions there are numberless school allotments for which no candidate could be found. In Illinois the teachers of these endowed schools, and there are few of any other class, except in large towns, do not assuredly make great pretensions to literary distinction. Happening to be one of a party at the examination of a candidate for the school-land near our house, I was surprised to see how easily the bonus was obtained; the reader will perhaps smile when he is told that the spelling book was the only standard by which his qualifications were tested; what may be expected from the pupils of such masters is left for the arithmetical capabilities of the reader to determine. I may, however, remark, that were it not for the influx of European emigrants and settlers from the more eastern states, all traces of a scientific nature would very soon disappear.

I have introduced this trait of character with a view to qualify the opinions which some of the foregoing facts might give rise to. In human nature, all the world over, there are certain bold mental and moral features, which, under similar training, seldom fail to shew themselves. I would by no means be understood to imply that ignorance and dishonesty are synonymous terms, or that an acquaintance with the arts and sciences prevents a person from being a knave. All that is here meant is included in the well-known statistical fact, that crime is the most prevalent where the attainments of society are of the lowest order. This is a truth which modern investigation has fully established, although the ancients were not ignorant concerning it.

"*Ingenuas didicisse fideliter artes*
Emollet mores, nec sinit esse feros."

The influence of christianity on the morals of mankind is considered sufficient without the aid of education to restrain vicious propensities. True christianity practically enjoyed, must, I am persuaded, make its possessor a good man and a good citizen. But I am equally certain that the blessings that accrue to society thence arising, bear a direct proportion to the state, as to intelligence, in which that society is found. For proofs of this assertion, I refer not to the experience of times gone by, when

"A second deluge learning over-ran,
And the monks finished what the Goths began."

I intend rather to make good my position by a short account of the religious peculiarities of the people whose character I am attempting to pourtray.

Prior to leaving England, I had been for nearly twenty years a member of the Wesleyan Methodist Society, and consequently felt wishful, as soon as our circumstances would allow, to join the religious body called the Methodists in that country. I attended a class meeting held in a house about two miles from our residence; but the manner in which it was conducted was by no means congenial to my views and sentiments. The company being assembled and seated, the one acting as leader, rose from his seat, which was a signal for the others to do the same. A sort of circle or ring was then immediately formed, by the whole assembly taking hold of hands, and capering about the house surprisingly. Their gesture could not be called dancing, and yet no term that I can employ describes it better. This done, worship commenced with extempore prayer, not indeed in language or style the best selected, but with this I have nothing to do. I have no right to question the sincerity of the individual, and if his taste differed from mine, it is no proof that his was wrong. The following part of the service was exceedingly exceptionable. All the persons present being again seated, an individual started from his

144

seat, exclaiming in a loud and frantic shriek, "I feel it," meaning what is commonly termed among them the power of God. His motions, which appeared half convulsive, were observed with animated joy by the rest, till he fell apparently stiff upon the floor, where he lay unmolested a short time, and then resumed his seat. Others were affected in a similar manner, only in some instances the power of speech was not suspended, as in this, by the vehemence of enthusiasm, for I cannot give it a more moderate name.

Finding in this mode of worship little that I could really respect, I resolved not long afterwards to absent myself from them altogether. I found moreover that some of the most rapturous members were far from being exemplary in their conduct, practically considered. As to their other forms of religious worship I have few remarks to offer. The Americans are fond of the word liberty; ✓ it is indeed the burden of their song, their glory, and their pride. In some respects this is praiseworthy—an essential ingredient in national honour and national greatness; but in my opinion it is carried too far when it enters the sanctuary. It may be pleasant to hear of religious bodies worshipping under their own vine and fig tree, in the manner best adapted to their views and feelings.

Views and feelings, it is well known, are dependent on educational precepts and original impressions. These therefore must vary, and experience shews they do vary proportionally to the endowments or discipline of the individual. And yet religion is only one, the gospel is only one; and consequently no two conflicting creeds can be both right. How far a person's private judgment ought to be at liberty to originate, select, or improve modes of faith and worship, I pretend not to determine. If it be a privilege which all classes of the community may claim with propriety, no consequences can be more natural than those which have hitherto thence arisen, viz: the continual appearance of new sects or denominations. Either from constitutional peculiarity or educational bias, the minds of mankind possess faculties for thinking and feeling too widely different for them ever to be consentaneous, especially in matters where much is left imperfectly defined, probably as a test of obedience and faith.

I have been led into this digression, because, on hearing some of the preachers in Illinois, I have often thought them out of their place when they have been attempting to substantiate whimsies of their own, rather than truths fairly deduced from the Word of God. The fact is, too little regard is paid either to the fitness of the preacher or the sanctity of the office. If an individual's inclinations prompt him to become a preacher, little or no further explanation is demanded. This, of course, can only be understood to refer to the thinly inhabited districts, where, I assure the reader, it is not necessary to be very fastidious, in order to find ample reason for doubting whether, under the name of religious worship, there is not a mixture of superstition and unhallowed excitement. Besides the usual Sabbath observances, camp meetings are frequently held in the open air. These are commonly termed two-day meetings, though they are frequently kept up the greater part of the week. They are attended by persons of different denominations, and conducted in a very irregular manner; one part of the assembly being on their knees, while another is listening to an exhortation from one of the preachers.

It is now requisite that I should once more resume my narrative. The reader is aware I do not pretend to preserve it unbroken to the present time. The greatest difficulties incident to emigrants, commonly occur at the commencement of their enterprising career; what our beginning was, has been explained in detail; it remains, therefore, only to describe our present condition. Before I can

properly effect this purpose, it will be necessary to state the particulars of that event
which induced me, once more, to visit the
shores of Old England; "my own sweet native earth." Mr. B., the reader has been informed, got married about four years after
our arrival; being an industrious and frugal
man, his affairs kept continually improving;
he put out, as loans, several hundred dollars,
for which he received good interest: his cattle, also, was numerous, from which he obtained a good livelihood, by keeping under
the plough as much land as grew them provender for winter. He lived, however, only a
few years; I shall never forget, poor man, the
last time he was at our house. I was rather
unwell; after seeing me he went round our
farm with my husband, and then called in
again to bid me good evening, saying, he
hoped I should be better when he came
again; but "how frail at best is dying man;"
that very night he began in the typhus fever,
which terminated his earthly existence in a
few days; he died childless and without will.

Being in regular correspondence with my
children in England, although I have till now
felt it my duty to be silent on that subject,
lest the reader should be entirely bewildered
with the recital of anxieties arising from so
many sources, I sent them an account of his

death, and wished them to name it to his
brother; this being done, the latter, who has
a large family in England, and is consequently anxious to better his condition, took
it into his head to visit the deceased's widow
in America, hoping to become entitled to some
of his property; accordingly he left his family to take care of his home, and in company
with another person wishful to emigrate,
sailed for New Orleans early in the present
year. Neither we, nor Mr. B.'s widow, were
aware of his coming; we were all taken by
surprise; well do I remember the first appearance of these two Yorkshiremen, who had
agreed to introduce themselves as strangers.
Little did we think when we saw them ram-
bling in our farm like two incurious travellers, that they were objects of such interest
to us as they proved to be; self and husband
were in the fields when they found us. I fan-
cied I perceived a likeness of the Mr. B., in
one of them, and challenged him as his
brother; I was right: silence confirmed the
conjecture, and we immediately invited them
into the house, and treated them with good
Old English hospitality, eagerly devouring
all the tidings we could elicit from them. I
dare say we were thought tediously inquisi-
tive, as we kept our guests in talk till after
midnight, before we allowed them to retire.

A True Picture of Emigration

The following day was spent in looking over our farm, and as the reader has been made acquainted with our difficulties, it is but just that he should know how we were situated on this occasion. In the first instance I may state that the house we at present occupy has been recently erected, and though in externals there is nothing to boast of, it is much superior to the one we occupied during former years. The situation itself is more airy and open. Our furniture is also more in accordance with modern times than that we occupied at the commencement of our career. The three-footed stools which then served as our ordinary seats, have long since been banished the house, and designated with the humble title of milking stools; and in short our house has been entirely re-furnished, and useful articles of various kinds have been procured. It is however not so much either in the house or its furniture that our success manifests itself: were these to be made the principal objects by which possessions are estimated, there are after all few cottagers in England that would not be on an equality with us, with this exception, theirs are generally rented, while ours is our own freehold. I may further observe, with reference to the furniture of our house, that we have for many years had abundance, and I might say a superabundance of those essentials of housekeeping, which, if not the most ornamental in a sitting room, are not the least valuable in a family; that is to say, we have known no lack of good food, such as beef, pork, butter, fowls, eggs, milk, flour, and fruits, all of which we have, as Yorkshire farmers say, within ourselves; but as I intimated before, our out-door possessions were the objects that chiefly engaged the attention of our guests. At this time we had at least twenty head of horned cattle, of which we kill or sell off some at every autumn; we have seven horses, including one or two foals; besides pigs, sheep, and poultry, the number of which I am not able to state as they keep continually breeding, and are never to be seen altogether. Our land, which is of excellent quality and very productive, pleased our visitants very much, who went round the greater part of it, although it extends to a great distance from our house, as we have by purchases made at sundry times three hundred and sixty acres, more than half of which is cultivated. Not wishing to manage the whole ourselves, we have two small farms let off, for which we receive as rent a dollar an acre. It is not difficult to let land broken up at the above rate. Many who do not possess the means for purchasing land, are glad to rent a few acres on which to grow provender for their cattle during winter, and food for themselves.

I wish to make no boast of our possessions; but having told the difficulties we experienced at our commencement, I ought in fairness to state what our success has been; I do this and no more; the lapse of a dozen years has wonderfully changed the appearance of things. We have seen a neighbourhood rise around us; and in some situations, where at our first coming, everything appeared in its native wildness, small villages have now begun to rise. Means of comfort are now within our reach. We remember the time when we knew not where to apply for an article if at all out of daily use; but by the increase of population, we can now easily obtain anything we require, either as food, physic, or clothing, and were we disposed to give up labour, we could live very comfortably on the fruits of our former toil. One thing I would notice as a cause of our ultimate prosperity, is, that having a family, we have been greatly assisted in the culture of our land, without having so much to hire as we should otherwise have been obliged. Were I asked what is my opinion respecting emigration, I would refer the enquirer to the foregoing narrative; here are facts, let him consider and judge for himself. If our success has been ultimately greater than at one time we anticipated, or even than that of many of our neighbours, as indeed it has, it must be borne in mind that our industry and perseverance have been unremitting. If our cattle and lands have kept increasing, that increase is but the reward for the numberless anxieties we have experienced, and the privations we have undergone. Few would undertake the latter to secure the former.

Before concluding my narrative, I beg to state that I do not sympathize with those who assert that to leave one's country and become an emigrant, implies a want of patriotism. There are a few facts bearing on this question which I may be allowed to mention. Is not, I would ask, the population of the United Kingdom as great at the present time as its means can comfortably support and employ, and if so, how would the mother country be able to maintain the millions now in America, that have sprung from her?

The soil and mineral productions of America are of the most valuable character:—rich in all that is calculated to make a community great, independent, and happy. The same all-bountiful parent that has given to Great Britain her vast resources, whereby her densely peopled towns, and villages scattered over a thousand hills derive subsistence, has been at work in America. Looking at the question in its more enlarged and true character, assuming that the entire earth is under the dominion of man, how can we suppose that some parts of England, whose natural character is sterility, should be brought under a barely remunerating culture, while there are millions of acres elsewhere, as productive as any soil on which the common orb of day has shone, still a wild uninhabited wilderness. These are questions to which time is giving and must give a proper answer, and in so doing the mother country itself will be no loser.

The greatness of England, it has been long understood, is dependent upon its manufactures and commerce, and if so, I would further ask what country has contributed so much to foster those manufactures and support that commerce as the United States of America? Thinking and feeling like one that is proud of her relation to England and that loves her own country, I consider it no disgrace to the British nation that I have travelled thousands of miles in America, from New Orleans to Illinois, and then thence on the Ohio by Cincinnati and Philadelphia to New York on my way home, that I have visited cities, some of which already number hundreds of thousands of inhabitants, and never found a place where using my own English tongue, I had any difficulty in making myself understood or of comprehending all I heard spoken.

But to complete my narrative. The object of one of our guests, as already explained, was to settle in the country. Not having sufficient money to establish himself as an occupier of land, he became a day-labourer with immediate employment. Being entirely unacquainted with the method of farming as practised in Illinois, his first wages were only fourteen dollars per month and his board. With this he appeared satisfied, and said he found things better than he anticipated. As to Mr. B.'s brother, his purpose was to obtain something from the widow of the deceased, to which he certainly had a legal claim. Finding that his share would be all in land (160 acres) he soon manifested signs of impatience to be going back to England for his wife and family in order to occupy it. The idea of a person leaving us to go direct to the country, on which a large share of my affections will ever be placed, increased the desire, which I had never ceased to indulge, of visiting once more the shores of Old England. The purpose thus suggested was weighed over with feelings such as the sensitive reader will not require me to explain. No feeble motives could have prompted me to take the step I am here describing; connected with the thought of coming to England, dear as it was, I saw I should have to cross the Atlantic twice during the remainder of the summer, besides much tedious inland travelling. It required me to resist the entreaties of my children, who, with tears in their eyes, daily urged me not to leave them. But I will not go through these sad details. I will not repeat the arguments my neighbours employed to induce me to stay: how they reminded me that old age was beginning to number me among its victims; that it was in vain for me to think I could do as I had done. My decisive reply to these and many other obstacles which comfort, prudence, maternal and conjugal love suggested, was, "it must be now or never."

Decided, therefore, to carry out the resolve to which I had come, I prepared to accompany our guest, and finally left Illinois for England on the 20th of April, where we arrived after a prosperous voyage on the 19th of June; and thus am I again, for a few short summer weeks, in my own country. I will not trouble the reader further with my story. If the account I have given of our proceedings, adverse and successful, does not allure his fancy with ideas of visionary prosperity as the invariable result of crossing the seas, it may perchance tend to make him a little better satisfied with his present condition, though it should only be a snug little cottage in the land where his childhood was reared. If it does this, it will be something— my purpose will be served—and thus, reader, I wish thee farewell.

NOTE.—The writer[1] feels it due to state that the subject of this narrative, as implied above, returned, after a stay in England of about three months, taking with her the daughter,[2] mentioned at the first outset as being left, the husband of the same, and their two children, besides a family or two of connections. Since their departure three or four other families from their own immediate neighbourhood have followed.

[1] Edward Burlend whose rôle in writing the narrative is recited in our Historical Introduction.

[2] Mary Burlend, the daughter alluded to on page 9 as remaining behind in England when the family migrated to America in 1831. On Feb. 10, 1840, she married, in her native Yorkshire, Luke Yelliott. In 1846 the Yelliotts followed the Burlends to Pike County, Illinois, where they established their permanent home, in which John and Rebecca Burlend were sheltered during their declining years. See *History of Pike County, Illinois* (Chicago, 1880), 444.

Index

Index

A Catechism of English History, author of, xxi.

Ague, afflicts settlers, 114.

Allen, Francis, I, husband of Sarah Burlend, 9.

Allen, Francis, II, aids editor, xxix–xxx, 64.

Amy Thornton; or the Curate's Daughter, author of, xxi.

Ants, of Illinois, described, 192.

Atlantic Ocean, emigrants cross, 14–32, 156–57; tempest on, 18–22; tedium of voyage, 22; beauty, 23; pirates on, 28–29.

Atlas, epidemic at, 64.

A True Picture of Emigration, authorship of, xxii–xxvii.

BARTER, in pioneer Illinois, 78–79.

Bay of Biscay, vessel driven to, 21.

Bees, incident narrated, 37.

Bethel Cemetery, burial place of English emigrants, xxvii–xxviii, 8–9; Burlend home near, 57.

Bethel church, Rebecca Burlend attends, xxviii.

Bickerdike, Charles, leads English migration to Pike County, 8, 41, 149–50, 155; characterized, 50–52; dealings with Burlends, 70, 74, 89, 118–19, 131; marriage, 123; death, 148.

Birds, of Illinois, described, 96–98.

Blacksnake, described, 99.

Boone family, settles in Scott County, 46.

Bread, Illinois method of making, 59–60.

Brevet, ——, misconduct related, 68–71.

British Museum, possesses works of Edward Burlend, xxi.

Buck, Prof. S. J., bibliography cited, xxiii.

Bull-frogs, described, 104–105.

Burlend, Charlotte, career, 9.

Index

Burlend, Edward, as author, xx–xxiv, 62, 157; intro-
    duces narrative, 5; remains in England, 9.
Burlend, Hannah, career, 9.
Burlend family, economic condition, 7; departure for
    America, 8–14; crosses Atlantic, 15–32; ascends
    Mississippi, 33–40; arrival in Pike County, 41–57;
    American career narrated, 58–157. See also the
    various members of the family.
Burlend, John, I, husband of Rebecca Burlend, xx;
    characterized, xxx; attitude toward migration to
    America, 7–15; rescues son, 27; foils robber, 39;
    seeks family shelter, 43–45, 50; contest with squat-
    ter, 68–69; as hunter, 73–74; injured, 89–92; tracks
    raccoon, 105; sells watch, 110; buys livestock,
    115–19; plants garden, 122; fights fire, 125–27; pur-
    chases land, 131–32; fights land jumper, 132–40;
    old-age home, xxix, 157.
Burlend, John, II, career, 9; daring, 27; aids parents,
    80; sympathy for father, 90.
Burlend (Yelliott), Mary, remains in England, 9; re-
    moval to America, xxix, 157; shelters parents,
    xxix–xxx, 157.
Burlend, Rebecca, as author, xviii–xx; revisits England,
    xxiv–xxv, 148, 155–57; burial place, xxvii; character-
    ized, xxviii–xxxi; attitude toward leaving England,
    7–15; farewell emotions, 16–17; describes tempests,
    18–22, 80–81; moonlight reflections, 23–24; ad-
    venture with fire, 26–27, 126–27; fondness for
    ocean vessel, 35–36; harvests maple sugar, 78;
    plants corn, 80; clears land, 87; harvests wheat,
    90–92; adventure with rattlesnake, 124–25; with
    land jumper, 134–38; religious views, 144–47; old-
    age home, xxix, 157.
Burlend, Sarah, career, 9.
Burland, William, career, 9.
Burns, ——, neighbor of Burlends, 70; extends aid,
    121–22, 129.

Index

Burton, Rebecca, see Rebecca Burlend.

Butterflies, of Illinois, described, 102.

Buzzard, as food, 73–74.

CAMP-MEETINGS, described, 147.

Carr, ——, land jumper, 132–39.

Cattle, method of rearing, 75–78, 130.

Cemeteries, Bethel, xxvii–xxviii, 8–9, 57; Swillington, xx–xxi.

Cheat-wheat, 106–107, 128.

Climate, of Illinois, described, 69–70, 80–82, 92–95, 104.

Commerce, of England, 16; of New Orleans, 34.

Copperheads, described, 99–100.

Corn meal, as food, 58–59.

DALBY, Thomas, husband of Hannah Burlend, 9.

Detroit, Burlend home near, xxviii, 57.

ELLEDGE, Elizabeth, inheritance of, 43; mother, 46.

England, emigrants remove to Illinois, xxvii, 8–14; farewell to, 16–17; sources of national strength, 154–55.

FARRAND, James, reports second edition of Burlend narrative, xxv.

Fences, rail, described, 72–73.

Ferries, see Philips Ferry.

Fire-flies, described, 103.

Flatboats, in Mississippi River trade, 34.

Flowers, of Illinois prairies, described, 84–85.

Furniture, described, 49, 64–65, 150–51.

GRIGGSVILLE, residents of, xxv, 9.

Gulf of Mexico, piracy in, 29.

Home, Burlends cross ocean on, 15–32, 35.

Hospitality, of Americans, 45–46; of Burlends, 74, 149–56.

ILLINOIS, bibliography of *Travel and Description*, xxiii; houses of settlers, 47–52; land system, 52–55, 131–40; bread-making, 59–60; climate, 69–70, 80–82, 92–95, 104; cattle-rearing, 75–78, 130;

mosquitoes, 82–83; prairies, 83–84; flowers, 85; trees, 85–86; birds, 96–98, 104; snakes, 99–101; insects, 101–102; animals, 104–106; threshing methods, 106–107; ague, 114; culture, 141–43; religious practices, 144–47.

Illinois mange, described, 63–64.

Illinois River, emigrants ascend, 40–42.

Illinois River Valley, as home of Burlends, xxviii; fertility, 62.

Indian corn, crop described, 60–63; planted, 79–80, 121–22; harvested, 109; damaged by freezing, 111.

Insects, of Illinois, described, 101–103.

Irish Channel, emigrants traverse, 18.

JACKSON, General Andrew, defense of New Orleans, 29.

KINZIE, Mrs. Juliette A., author of *Lakeside Classics* volume, xvii–xviii.

Knowles, ——, dealings with Burlends, 110, 129.

Lakeside Classics, authors of, xvii; list of volumes published, 169.

Land, system in Illinois, 52–55, 131–40; method of clearing, 86–87.

Leeds, sale of Burlend narrative in, xxvii.

Liberty, religious, abuse of, 145–47.

Library of Congress, lacks Burlend data, xxi.

Lighting, pioneer methods described, 65–66.

Lightning, display of, in Illinois, 80–82.

Lincoln, Abraham, visits New Orleans, 34.

Liverpool, stay of Burlends in, 9–14.

Log houses, described, 47–52.

MAPLE trees, sugar-making described, 55; sugar harvested, 78, 120–21, 131.

Matanuska, emigrants mentioned, xix.

Medicine, Rebecca Burlend practices, xxix–xxx.

Methodists, religious services of, 144–45.

Mills, laws governing erection of, 139–41.

Mississippi River, route via, 15, 35; emigrants ascend, 31, 35–41; fuel used by steamers, 36.

Index

Missouri River, characterized, 38.

Mosquitoes, among settlers, 82–83.

NEGROES, bee-hive incident, 36–37; thief, 39. See also
Slavery.

New Orleans, route via, 15; Andrew Jackson defends,
29; emigrants reach, 31–32; described, 33–34; as
market for interior produce, 67.

Noises, of Illinois nighttime, described, 104–105.

OAKES, ——, Pike County squatter, xxviii; sells pre-
emption right, 54–57; livestock, 59–60, 68.

Ohio River characterized, 38.

PADDOCK, ——, neighbor of Burlends, 59, 70; sells
emption right, 131–32.

Philips, Andrew, owns ferry, 42–43.

Philips, Asa, inheritance of, 43.

Philips (Norris), Nancy, inheritance of, 42–43; characterized, 45–46.

Philips, Nimrod, career, 42–43; defends Burlends,
140–41.

Philips, Selah, inheritance of, 43.

Philips, Zerrelda Jean, inheritance of, 42–43.

Philips Ferry, arrival of Burlends at, 41–44. See also
Valley City.

Pike County, as home of Burlends, xxiv; English
migration to, xxv–xxvii, xxxi, 8; epidemic in, 64.

Pike County Republican, cited, 9.

Piracy, encountered, 28–29.

Pittsfield, home of Burlend descendants, xxi, xxiii–xxv,
xxix.

Potatoes, raised, 111.

Prairies, described, 83–84.

Preëmptions, explained, 53; conflict over, 131–39.

QUINCY, land office at, 135.

RACCOONS, described, 105–106.

Racer, see Blacksnake.

Rattlesnakes, described, 100–101; encounter with,
124–25.

Index

Religion, status of, in Pike County, 71; services described, 144–47.

Rhodes, Albert, remembers Rebecca Burlend, xxx.

SABBATH, disregard of in New Orleans, 33; Burlends observe, 71.

St. Louis, route via, 35; growth, 40–41.

Salt, fondness of cattle for, 76–77.

Schools, government endows, 141–42.

School teachers, educational standards, 142.

Scott County, Boones settle in, 46.

Sea-sickness, afflicts emigrants, 18.

Skillet, use, described, 59.

Slavery, at New Orleans, 33–34; on lower Mississippi, 36.

Snakes, of Illinois, described, 99–101.

Soap, pioneer method of making, 66–67.

Squatters, in Illinois, mentioned, xxviii; rôle explained, 54; misconduct, 68–69.

Stores, pioneer, described, 67–78; operations, 78–79, 88, 107–108, 129.

Sugar, see Maple trees.

Sulphur, as remedy for Illinois mange, 63–64.

Sumac tree, described, 55–56.

Swillington, home of Edward Burlend, xx.

TEMPESTS, described, 18–22, 80–81.

The Wesleyan Emigrants, see *A True Picture of Emigration*.

Thief, attempts robbery, 39.

Thompson, Jess M., owns copy of *Village Rhymes*, xxi; on authorship of *True Picture of Emigration*, xxiii–xxiv; as source of information, xxv, 9, 54, 64, 115.

Tillson, Mrs. Christiana H., author of *Lakeside Classics* volume, xvii–xviii.

Trees, varieties encountered on Mississippi, 37–38; impede navigation, 38; of Illinois, described, 85–86; destroyed, 86–87, 122–23.

Index

Turkey buzzard, as food, 73–74.

VALLEY City, Burlend home near, xxviii, 57. See also Philips Ferry.

Van Dusen (Vanderoozen), Garret, establishes ferry, 42; sells livestock, 115–18, 129.

Varley, —, pioneer storekeeper, 78–79, 88, 107–108, 129.

Venison, as food, 54, 59.

Village Rhymes, authorship of, xx–xxii.

WEATHER, see climate.

West Indies, emigrants traverse, 27–30.

Whalen, Hazel, supplies information, xxv–xxvi.

Wheat, harvested, 89–92, 123–24, 128, 131; threshed, 106–107; sold, 107–108; sowed, 109–110; field burned, 125–27.

Whetstones, needed, 123.

Whip-poor-wills, described, 104.

Winters, of Illinois, described, 69–70.

Wolves, prevalence of, 70.

Women, as authors of *Lakeside Classics*, xvii–xviii.

YELLIOTT, Luke, husband of Mary Burlend, 157; see also Mary Burlend.

Yellow fever, afflicts New Orleans, 34.

Yorkshire, home of Burlends, xviii–xx, 5, 7, 9; Rebecca Burlend revisits, xxiv–xxv, 155–57; families migrate to Illinois, xxxi, 157.